I0426290

May 2012

VETERANS' PENSION BENEFITS

Improvements Needed to Ensure Only Qualified Veterans and Survivors Receive Benefits

Accountability ★ Integrity ★ Reliability

May 2012

VETERANS' PENSION BENEFITS

Improvements Needed to Ensure Only Qualified Veterans and Survivors Receive Benefits

Highlights of GAO-12-540, a report to congressional requesters

Why GAO Did This Study

The VA pension program is intended to provide economic benefits to wartime veterans and survivors with financial need. GAO was asked to examine (1) how the design and management of VA's pension program ensure that only those with financial need receive pension benefits and (2) what is known about organizations that are marketing financial products and services to enable veterans and survivors to qualify for VA pension benefits. GAO's study included a review of VA's policies and procedures, site visits to VA's three Pension Management Centers, and online research and interviews of organizations that market financial and estate planning services to help veterans and survivors qualify for VA pension benefits.

What GAO Recommends

Congress should consider establishing a look-back and penalty period for pension claimants who transfer assets for less than fair market value prior to applying, similar to other federally supported means-tested programs. VA should (1) request information about asset transfers and other assets and income sources on application forms, (2) verify financial information during the initial claims process, (3) strengthen coordination with VA's fiduciary program, and (4) provide clearer guidance to claims processors assessing claimants' eligibility. In its comments on this report, VA concurred with three of GAO's recommendations and concurred in principle with one, citing concerns about the potential burden on claimants and recipients of verifying reported financial information. VA agreed to study the issue further.

View GAO-12-540. View related video clip. For more information, contact Daniel Bertoni at (202) 512-7215 or bertonid@gao.gov.

What GAO Found

The Department of Veterans Affairs' (VA) pension program design and management do not adequately ensure that only veterans with financial need receive pension benefits. While the pension program is means tested, there is no prohibition on transferring assets prior to applying for benefits. Other means-tested programs, such as Medicaid, conduct a look-back review to determine if an individual has transferred assets at less than fair market value, and if so, may deny benefits for a period of time, known as the penalty period. This control helps ensure that only those in financial need receive benefits. In contrast, VA pension claimants can transfer assets for less than fair market value immediately prior to applying and be approved for benefits. For example, GAO identified a case where a claimant transferred over a million dollars less than 3 months prior to applying and was granted benefits. Also, VA's process for assessing initial eligibility is inadequate in several key respects. The application form does not ask for some sources of income and assets such as private retirement income, annuities, and trusts. As a result, VA lacks complete information on a claimant's financial situation. Also, the form does not ask about asset transfers—information VA needs to determine whether these assets should be included when assessing eligibility. In addition, VA does not verify all the information it does request on the form. For example, VA does not routinely request supporting documents, such as bank statements or tax records, unless questions are raised. VA's fiduciary program, which appoints individuals to manage the financial affairs of beneficiaries who are unable to do so themselves, collects financial information that may affect some pension recipients' eligibility, but VA pension claims processors do not have access to all this information. Further, guidance on when assets should be included as part of a claimant's net worth is unclear; and VA claims processors must use their own discretion when assessing eligibility for benefits, which can lead to inconsistent decisions.

GAO identified over 200 organizations that market financial and estate planning services to help pension claimants with excess assets meet financial eligibility requirements for these benefits. These organizations consist primarily of financial planners and attorneys who offer products such as annuities and trusts. GAO judgmentally selected a nongeneralizable sample of 25 organizations, and GAO investigative staff successfully contacted 19 while posing as a veteran's son seeking information on these services. All 19 said a claimant can qualify for pension benefits by transferring assets before applying, which is permitted under the program. Two organization representatives said they helped pension claimants with substantial assets, including millionaires, obtain VA's approval for benefits. About half of the organizations advised repositioning assets into a trust, with a family member as the trustee to direct the funds to pay for the veteran's expenses. About half also advised placing assets into some type of annuity. Some products and services provided, such as deferred annuities, may not be suitable for the elderly because they may not have access to all their funds for their care within their expected lifetime without facing high withdrawal fees. Also, these products and services may result in ineligibility for Medicaid for a period of time. Among the 19 organizations contacted, the majority charged fees, ranging from a few hundred dollars for benefits counseling to $10,000 for establishment of a trust.

_____ United States Government Accountability Office

Contents

Abbreviations

EVR	Eligibility Verification Report
IVM	Income Verification Match
PMC	Pension Management Centers
SSA	Social Security Administration
SSI	Supplemental Security Income
VA	Department of Veterans Affairs
VBA	Veterans Benefits Administration

View GAO Components

Video: Examples of Messages from Companies about Transferring Assets to Qualify for VA Pension Benefits

United States Government Accountability Office
Washington, DC 20548

May 15, 2012

The Honorable Patty Murray
Chairman
The Honorable Richard Burr
Ranking Member
Committee on Veterans' Affairs
United States Senate

The Honorable Herb Kohl
Chairman
Special Committee on Aging
United States Senate

The Honorable Ron Wyden
United States Senate

The Department of Veterans Affairs' (VA) pension program is intended to provide economic benefits to wartime veterans with financial need. It is available to veterans who are age 65 and older or who have disabilities that are unrelated to their military service, as well as to their surviving spouses and dependent children. To be eligible for VA pension benefits, a claimant must meet certain income and asset requirements. Recently, concerns have been raised that some organizations are marketing financial products and other services to enable claimants whose assets exceed the pension program's financial eligibility thresholds to qualify for these benefits. Also, these organizations may charge substantial fees for products and services that may not always be in claimants' best long-term interests.

At your request, we reviewed VA's pension program. Specifically, we examined (1) how the design and management of VA's pension program ensure that only those with financial need receive pension benefits, and (2) what is known about organizations that are marketing financial products and services to veterans and survivors to enable them to qualify for VA pension benefits. To address our first objective, we reviewed relevant federal laws and regulations, as well as policies and procedures regarding how VA assesses financial eligibility for pension benefits. We interviewed officials from VA headquarters, as well as staff at VA's three Pension Management Centers (PMC) to determine how these policies and procedures are applied. We also reviewed a nongeneralizable random sample of 85 pension claims that were entered into VA's electronic case file system in fiscal year 2010, in which VA had to formally determine if the claimant met asset thresholds.[1] To address our second objective, we conducted internet research and interviews with veterans' advocacy groups, VA officials, and state and local officials to identify organizations that market financial and estate planning services to help veterans and surviving spouses qualify for VA pension benefits. We contacted some of these organizations to obtain their views on the types and suitability of the products and services they provide. In addition, we judgmentally selected 25 organizations to contact where our investigative staff posed as the son of an 86-year-old veteran, to obtain first-hand information about the types of products and services provided, and associated costs for a potential pension claimant. The 25 organizations were judgmentally selected to achieve geographic dispersion and include both financial planners and attorneys. Based on availability, we had discussions with representatives of 19 of these organizations.

We conducted this performance audit from July 2011 to May 2012 in accordance with generally accepted government auditing standards. These standards require that we plan and perform the audit to obtain sufficient, appropriate evidence to provide a reasonable basis for our findings and conclusions based on our audit objectives. We believe that the evidence obtained provides a reasonable basis for our findings and conclusions based on our audit objectives. Additional information on our scope and methodology is provided in appendix I.

Background

In fiscal year 2011, VA provided about $ 4.3 billion in pension benefits for about 517,000 recipients. These benefits are available to low-income wartime veterans who are age 65 and older, or who are under age 65 but are permanently and totally disabled as a result of conditions unrelated to their military service.[2] Surviving spouses and dependent children may also be eligible for these benefits. At the end of fiscal year 2011, about

---

[1]Our sample was nongeneralizable because not all pension claims where VA had to determine if the claimant met asset thresholds had been entered into VA's electronic case file system in fiscal year 2010.

[2]VA currently administers three pension programs, commonly referred to as Improved Law Pensions (Pub. L. No. 95-588, 92 Stat. 2497), Prior Law Pensions (Pub. L. No. 86-211, 73 Stat. 432), and Old Law Pensions (Pub. L. No. 73-2, 48 Stat. 8). About 95 percent of all pension recipients are under the Improved Pension program, and new beneficiaries can only accede to this program. We will focus on the Improved Pension program in this report. For veterans with service-connected disabilities, VA provides cash benefits through its disability compensation program.

314,000 pension recipients were veterans and about 203,000 were survivors. Also, about 329,000 recipients were over 65 and the average age was 71 for veterans and 79 for survivors. Average annual payments in fiscal year 2011 were $9,669 for veterans and $6,209 for survivors.

VA provides pension benefits through its Veterans Benefits Administration (VBA), and accredits representatives of veterans' service organizations, attorneys, and claims agents to assist claimants with the preparation and submission of VA claims at no charge.[3] To become accredited, an individual must meet certain requirements set forth in federal law.[4] Claims processors assess claims at VBA's three Pension Management Centers (PMC) in Philadelphia, Penn.; Milwaukee, Wis.; and Saint Paul, Minn. As part of the pension program, VA provides enhanced pension benefit amounts to veterans and surviving family members who demonstrate the need for aid and attendance, or who are considered permanently housebound.[5] For pension beneficiaries who are deemed unable to manage their affairs due to mental impairments, VA appoints a fiduciary to manage the beneficiary's finances.

To qualify for pension benefits, claimants' countable income must not exceed annual pension limits that are set by statute. These income limits are also the maximum annual pension payment that a beneficiary may receive. Such limits may vary based on whether claimants are veterans or survivors and their family composition, as well as whether claimants need aid and attendance or are considered housebound. For example, to qualify for pension benefits in 2012, a veteran with no dependents and who is in need of Aid and Attendance benefits cannot have income that exceeds $20,447, while a surviving spouse in similar circumstances

---

[3]See 38 U.S.C. §§ 5901-5904.

[4]Id.

[5]Veterans may be eligible for Aid and Attendance benefits if they demonstrate an inability to perform everyday personal functions such as bathing, dressing, eating, adjusting prosthetic devices, and protecting themselves from hazards or dangers in their daily environment. They may also be eligible for these benefits if they are a patient in a nursing home, bedridden, or are blind or nearly blind. Veterans may be eligible for Housebound benefits if they have a disability rated at 100 percent and, as a result, are permanently or substantially confined to their homes, or have a disability rated at 100 percent and at least one other disability rated at 60 percent or more (although these individuals are legally classified as housebound, they may be able to leave their homes). See GAO, *VA Enhanced Monthly Benefits: Recipient Population Is Changing, and Awareness Could Be Improved*, GAO-12-153 (Washington, D.C.: Dec. 14, 2011).

cannot have an income that exceeds $13,138. In determining if a claimant's income is below program thresholds, VA includes recurring sources of income such as the Social Security Administration's (SSA) retirement and disability benefits, but not income from public assistance programs such as Supplemental Security Income (SSI). VA also allows some expenses, such as certain unreimbursed medical expenses that exceed 5 percent of the maximum pension amount the claimant is eligible for, to be deducted from a claimant's countable income. The annual amount pension beneficiaries receive is the difference between their countable income and the maximum pension amount they would be eligible for (see table 1).[6]

Table 1: 2012 Maximum Annual Pension Benefit Limits

Type of benefit	Limit for veteran with no dependents	Limit for veteran with one dependent	Limit for surviving spouse with no dependents	Limit for surviving spouse with one dependent
Pension without Aid and Attendance or Housebound benefit	$12,256	$16,051	$8,219	$10,759
Pension with Housebound benefit	14,978	18,773	10,046	12,582
Pension with Aid and Attendance benefit	20,447	24,239	13,138	15,673

Source: GAO analysis of information from VA website.

VA's policy manual specifically states that the pension program is not intended to protect substantial assets or preserve an estate for a beneficiary's heirs. In assessing financial eligibility for pension benefits, VA also considers net worth or the total value of claimants' assets, such as bank accounts, stocks, bonds, mutual funds, and any property other than the claimant's dwelling, a reasonable lot area, a vehicle, and personal belongings.[7] There are no thresholds on the value of a

---

[6]Certain veterans who receive nursing home or domiciliary care at the government's expense are only eligible for no more than $90.00 per month in pension benefits.

[7]See 38 C.F.R. § 3.275. For claimants who are veterans, VA also assesses the net worth of the veteran's spouse to determine financial eligibility.

claimant's assets that are defined in statute.[8] However, according to VA's procedures manual, claims processors are generally required to formally determine if claimants with assets worth over $80,000 have financial resources that will last a reasonable period of time to pay for their basic expenses. In making this determination, claims processors consider net worth, income, expenses, age, and life expectancy to determine if claimants' financial resources are sufficient to pay for their expenses without assistance from VA. Ongoing eligibility for pension recipients who previously reported any income other than, or in addition to, Social Security income is also assessed. These recipients must complete an annual Eligibility Verification Report (EVR), which requests information on income and assets, that is used to determine if recipients continue to be financially eligible for the pension program.[9]

Potential VA pension recipients may also be eligible for other means-tested programs. For example, they may be eligible for Medicaid, a joint federal-state health care financing program that provides coverage for long-term care services for certain individuals whose income and resources do not exceed specific thresholds. Each state administers its Medicaid program and establishes specific income and resource eligibility requirements that must fall within federal standards, but we reported in 2007 that in most states, an individual must have $2,000 or less in countable financial resources to be eligible.[10] Similarly, the SSI program provides cash benefits to individuals who are age 65 or older, blind, or disabled, and who have limited income and whose financial resources are $2,000 or less ($3,000 if the individual lives with their spouse).[11]

---

[8]The relevant statute states that a veteran's pension shall be denied "when the corpus of the estate of the veteran or, if the veteran has a spouse, the corpus of the estates of the veteran and of the veteran's spouse is such that under all the circumstances, including consideration of the annual income of the veteran, the veteran's spouse, and the veteran's children, it is reasonable that some part of the corpus of such estates be consumed for the veteran's maintenance." 38 U.S.C. § 1522(a).

[9]38 C.F.R. § 3.277.

[10]GAO, *Medicaid Long-Term Care: Few Transferred Assets before Applying for Nursing Home Coverage; Impact of Deficit Reduction Act on Eligibility Is Uncertain*, GAO-07-280 (Washington, D.C.: Mar. 26, 2007).

[11]Individuals in some states who require long-term care services can become eligible for Medicaid benefits through participation in the SSI program.

VA Pension Program Design and Management Do Not Ensure Only Those with Financial Need Receive Benefits

Program Allows Claimants to Transfer Assets Prior to Applying, Unlike Other Means-Tested Programs

We found several potential vulnerabilities in the VA pension program's design, as well as in VA's policies and procedures, that hinder the department's ability to ensure that only those in financial need receive benefits. More specifically, the program allows claimants to transfer assets prior to applying for benefits, and VA lacks complete information on claimants' finances, relies on self-reported information, and does not utilize all opportunities for coordination within the agency. Additionally, guidance that claims processors use may be unclear. Despite being means-tested, the program currently permits VA pension claimants to transfer assets and reduce their net worth prior to applying for these benefits.[12] Federal regulations state that, when evaluating financial eligibility for pension benefits, assets gifted to someone that does not reside in the claimant's household will reduce the claimant's net worth if all rights of ownership and control of the assets have been relinquished.[13] As a result, prior to applying for benefits, claimants can transfer excess assets to someone outside their household to meet the financial eligibility criteria for VA pension benefits and be approved, as long as they no longer retain ownership or control of the assets.[14] For example, we identified a case involving a pension recipient who transferred over a million dollars in assets into an irrevocable trust less than 3 months prior to applying for these benefits.[15] VA was aware of the asset transfer when

---

[12]38 C.F.R. § 3.276(b).

[13]Id.

[14]Assets gifted to a family member in the pension claimant's household do not reduce the claimant's net worth.

[15]An irrevocable trust is one that cannot be terminated by the individual who set up the trust once it is created. Black's Law Dictionary (8th ed. 2004).

this pension claim was approved and did not count the trust as part of the claimant's net worth. Although these types of transfers are generally permitted under law for the pension program, this practice is not consistent with other federal means-tested programs and weakens the pension program's goal of supporting those with financial need.

In contrast, for Medicaid—another means tested program—federal law explicitly restricts eligibility for coverage for long term care for certain individuals who transfer assets for less than fair market value prior to applying.[16,17] As a result, when an individual applies for Medicaid coverage for long-term care, states conduct a look-back—a review to determine if the applicant transferred assets for less than fair market value prior to applying. Individuals who transfer assets for less than fair market value during the 60 months prior to applying may be denied eligibility for long-term care coverage for a period of time, known as the penalty period.[18] For example, gifting assets would generally be considered a transfer of assets at less than fair market value and would result in a penalty period. Also, under the SSI program, claimants who transfer assets for less than fair market value prior to applying may become ineligible for these benefits for up to 36 months.[19]

---

[16]42 U.S.C. § 1396p(c).

[17]An asset transfer at less than fair market value would occur when the claimant gifts or sells a resource and gets in return an amount that is less than the value of the resource on the open market at the time of the transfer.

[18]The penalty period is calculated by dividing the uncompensated dollar value of the assets transferred by the average monthly cost of private nursing home care in the state (or in the community, at the option of the state). The penalty period generally begins on the later of (1) the first day of the month during or after which the individual transferred assets at less than fair market value, or (2) the date on which the individual would have been eligible for Medicaid coverage for long-term care if it were not for these asset transfers. Certain asset transfers are exempt from Medicaid penalty provisions such as a home transferred to an individual's spouse or disabled child. Asset transfers would also not be penalized if the individual can demonstrate that the transfer was carried out exclusively for purposes other than qualifying for Medicaid, or when the state determines that the penalty would result in undue hardship. 42 U.S.C. § 1396p(c).

[19]42 U.S.C. § 1382b(c)(1)(A).

VA Lacks Complete Information on Claimants' Finances

VA lacks complete information on claimants' finances because the forms used to assess financial eligibility do not prompt applicants to report certain types of income and asset information. While the instructions on the pension application forms ask claimants to report all income sources and assets they own,[20] the forms do not provide spaces for claimants to report some types of income and assets. For example, even though elderly pension claimants may receive private monthly retirement income, such as income from a company's retirement plan, the application forms do not specifically provide space for claimants to report such income. According to SSA, in 2009, 9 percent of the aggregate income of those age 65 and older consisted of private pension income.[21]

The application forms do provide a space to report other income sources not specifically itemized on the forms. However, some claims processors we spoke with said claimants who report an amount in that space do not usually specify the source of this income, or if this amount represents a single or a combination of income sources. As a result, they have to follow up with the claimant to obtain this information, which delays the processing of these claims.

Similarly, although the application forms specifically ask claimants to report assets such as bank accounts, stocks, and real property, the forms do not ask about other common assets such as annuities and trusts, which need to be considered when VA assesses claimants' financial eligibility. (See figure 1 to view the section of the application form pertaining to income and assets.)[22] We found cases where claimants did not report assets that they are not specifically asked to report. For example, in one case a claimant did not report a trust with assets valued at about $575,000. In another case, a claimant did not report a trust worth

---

[20]VA has one pension application form for veterans and another form for surviving spouses and dependents.

[21]Social Security Administration, *Fast Facts and Figures about Social Security 2011* (Washington D.C.: August 2011).

[22]An annuity is a financial instrument that provides income over a defined period of time for an initial payment of principal. An immediate annuity provides income immediately after the initial lump-sum payment. For a deferred annuity, the initial investment accumulates interest over a specified period of time before payments begin to be received. A trust is an arrangement in which a grantor transfers property to a trustee with the intention that it be held, managed, or administered by the trustee for the benefit of the grantor or certain designated individuals.

about $612,000. In contrast, we reviewed several state application forms for Medicaid long-term care benefits that specifically asked individuals to report information about annuities and trusts they may own, as well as retirement income.

Figure 1: Section of Application Form Pertaining to Income and Assets

VA form 21-526 (page 8)

Net worth section

ITEM NO.	SOURCES OF RECURRING MONTHLY INCOME
35A.	Social Security
35B.	U.S. Civil Service
35C.	U.S. Railroad Retirement
35D.	Military Retired Pay
35E.	Black Lung Benefits
35F.	Other (Interest, dividends, or one-time payments)

Monthly income section

NOTE: For Items 37A-37F provid

ITEM NO.	SOURCE	VE
37A.	Cash, non-interest bearing bank accounts	
37B.	Interest bearing bank accounts, certificates of deposit (CDs)	
37C.	Retirement accounts (IRAs, Keogh Plans, etc.)	
37D.	Stocks, bonds, and mutual funds	
37E.	Value of business assets	
37F.	Real property (not your home)	

Form 21-526 seeks financial data on five specific sources of monthly income and six sources of the applicant's net worth, but it makes no mention of private retirement income, annuities, or trusts.

Source: GAO analysis of VA documents.

VA's application forms also do not provide a specific space for claimants to report asset transfers, even though the instructions on the veterans' application form ask claimants to disclose this information. Asset transfers to someone outside the claimant's household are allowed under the pension program, as long as the claimant relinquishes ownership and control of the asset. However, VA still needs to know about any asset transfers when assessing a claimant's financial eligibility because, consistent with VA's regulations, the department must determine whether the claimant retains ownership and control of the transferred asset and if this asset should be counted as part of the claimant's net worth. Without a designated space to report this type of information, claimants may not report asset transfers on the application forms. For example, we saw one case where a veteran transferred assets worth about $500,000 into an irrevocable trust 2 weeks prior to applying and did not report this on the application. VA learned of this asset transfer because the claims processor inquired about how the claimant's medical expenses were being paid. If the claims processor had not identified these assets and determined that they should be included in the claimant's net worth, because the claimant had not relinquished all ownership and control, the claim could have been approved. Application forms that do not specifically request information about certain income sources and assets, as well as asset transfers, may prevent VA from obtaining complete information about claimants' financial situation to properly assess their eligibility for pension benefits.

VA Relies on Self-Reported Information, and Verification Processes Are Incomplete

When assessing pension claimants' eligibility, VA relies primarily on self-reported financial information that, unlike other means-tested programs, is not independently verified.[23] VA does not require claimants to submit documents that corroborate self-reported financial information with their application, such as bank statements and tax returns. VA also does not require receipts to verify some types of claimed deductible expenses, even though these expenses may be a factor that enables some pension claimants to qualify for benefits. Without independent verification of self-reported financial information, VA will have difficulty detecting fraudulent claims. We identified cases where VA found individuals were advised by third parties to claim expenses they did not incur related to assistance with everyday living activities. For example, we saw one claim that was prepared by a financial planner in which $1,700 in monthly caregiver payments to a daughter were claimed. The claimant subsequently stated to VA that he did not pay his daughter any caregiver fees. In another case, a pension recipient claimed an attorney advised him to claim he was paying his son $1,000 per month for services that were not being provided in order to be eligible for a higher pension rate. The recipient

---

[23]We reported a similar finding in GAO, *Veterans Benefits: Improved Management Would Enhance VA's Pension Program*, GAO-08-112 (Washington D.C.: Feb. 14, 2008).

subsequently withdrew this claimed medical expense. Most claims processors we spoke with said they accept self-reported financial information unless questions arise, and in those cases, supporting documentation may be requested. In contrast, some state Medicaid programs and the SSI program require applicants to submit documents that support some reported financial information, such as bank statements and tax returns.

VA also does not make use of existing opportunities to verify self-reported financial information during the initial eligibility determination. For example, VA conducts computer matches to verify reported income from SSA benefits during the initial claims assessment process but is not using this type of technology to verify the accuracy of other self-reported financial information. Additional automated systems may be available that would enable VA to independently verify financial information during the initial eligibility assessment. For example, while VA performs a data match with Internal Revenue Service and SSA data to assess ongoing eligibility, it does not perform this match at the time of the initial claims assessment. In addition, for the SSI program, SSA recently implemented the Access to Financial Institutions system that allows the program to electronically request and receive records from financial institutions and verify an applicant's or recipient's financial information. Similarly, Medicaid requires states to implement an asset verification system for assessing applicants' and recipients' financial eligibility.[24]

VA's efforts to verify ongoing eligibility for pension benefits also have some shortcomings. Pension recipients who have previously reported income in addition to, or other than, Social Security income must annually complete an EVR. However, like the application forms, the EVRs do not provide spaces for claimants to report private retirement income, annuities, trusts, or asset transfers, and self-reported financial information is not independently verified unless the claims processor has questions. In addition, because not all pension recipients complete an EVR, VA may not be able to identify potential changes in the financial situation of recipients that may affect their ongoing eligibility for these benefits.

Other efforts to verify ongoing eligibility may not be effective in identifying ineligible pension recipients. VA's Income Verification Match (IVM)

---

[24]42 U.S.C. § 1396w.

program uses a computer match to compare income reported to VA by pension recipients for a given year with SSA earned income data and IRS unearned income data for that year, to determine if these recipients have any unreported income. However, there is about a 15-month lag between when a pension recipient reports income and when the IVM can be conducted, and the delay may be even longer. For example, in 2011, VA was completing IVMs for income information that was reported in 2007. As a result, improper payments may be made to ineligible pension recipients for at least over a year, but possibly several years, before the error is detected. In one case we reviewed, a beneficiary, who was approved for benefits in 2004 and reported $900 in net worth when he applied, had stocks worth over $162,000 at that time, which was only identified through the IVM process in 2007. This created an overpayment of over $18,000 that VA eventually waived.[25] In addition to the IVM not being conducted in a timely manner, the match does not identify any assets that do not generate income, such as deferred annuities for which payments have not begun. Therefore, the IVM would not be effective in identifying these types of assets. Ultimately, delays in the IVM process prevent VA from promptly detecting improper pension payments and increase the magnitude of these payments.

Opportunities for Internal Coordination Are Not Maximized

Opportunities for coordination between VA's pension and fiduciary programs to identify ineligible pension recipients are not always maximized.[26] According to VA officials, over half of VA beneficiaries in the fiduciary program are pension recipients. Field examiners in this program visit beneficiaries and fiduciaries, and prepare reports that may contain financial information of some pension recipients. Claims processors had access to these reports, but VA issued guidance in July 2011 that restricts pension claims processors from accessing them in VA's electronic case file system. VA determined that claims processors did not need to review fiduciary program reports as part of their daily work. This guidance was issued due to concerns about the privacy of fiduciaries' personal information, and concerns that pension recipients in the fiduciary

---

[25]VA regulations set forth that overpayments will not be collected when it is determined that collection would be "against equity and good conscience." 38 C.F.R. § 1.962.

[26]VA's fiduciary program appoints and monitors third parties to help manage and protect the funds of VA beneficiaries who are unable to manage their own affairs due to mental impairments. Fiduciaries can be a spouse or other family member, or an entity such as a law firm, hospital, or nursing home. See 38 U.S.C. § 5502.

program were being put under greater scrutiny. However, fiduciary field exam reports may contain information on beneficiaries' finances that could be useful for claims processors in assessing eligibility for pension benefits. While safeguarding fiduciaries' personal information is important, access to these reports allows claims processors to obtain a more accurate picture of a beneficiary's financial situation. As a result, critical information to identify potentially ineligible individuals is not received, which may result in improper payments. Fiduciary program staff must notify the pertinent PMC when they identify information that may affect the ongoing eligibility of a pension recipient for these benefits, such as changes in a recipient's income and assets. Claims processors generally rely on notification from fiduciary program staff about possible financial ineligibility of pension beneficiaries, since these claims processors no longer have direct access to those documents. A VA official from one of the PMCs told us that when claims processors had access to field exam reports prior to the issuance of the new guidance, cases of asset transfers or unreported assets were identified from reviews of these reports, even when there was no prior notification from fiduciary program staff. In addition, as part of our case file review, we identified cases of asset transfers or unreported assets that were identified in fiduciary field exam reports. Without access to field exam reports from the fiduciary program, claims processors may not have all available information to assess an individual's financial eligibility.

Unclear Guidance on Assessing Financial Eligibility May Lead to Inconsistent Decisions

VA's guidance to claims processors on assessing financial eligibility for VA pension benefits is unclear about when certain assets should be counted as part of an applicant's net worth. As a result, claims processors may make inconsistent eligibility decisions. For example, VA's procedures manual states that the value of any property owned by pension claimants must be considered when assessing financial eligibility for benefits, but the manual does not specifically discuss when or under what circumstance annuities or trusts should count as part of net worth. According to VA officials, and consistent with VA regulations, the decision as to whether an asset should be counted in a claimant's net worth depends on whether the claimant has ownership and control of the asset. However, VA has not adequately defined the concept of ownership and control of assets in either its regulations or internal guidance and policy documents. As a result, VA cannot ensure that claims processors are making fully informed eligibility decisions that are consistent with VA policy.

Several claims processors we spoke with confirmed that guidance on assessing net worth is unclear, and that it is difficult to determine when to count certain assets. For example, one claims processor expressed uncertainty whether to count trusts established for children residing outside of a claimant's household when the funds are being used to pay for claimant's expenses, since VA's regulations do not directly address these types of cases. A VA official acknowledged that guidance on what constitutes ownership and control of an asset could be improved. We were provided local training material from one PMC on when to count assets in a trust and found that it seemed inconsistent with VA's regulations regarding when to count assets. For example, the PMC training material stated that a claim involving assets transferred into a trust a claimant cannot access would likely be denied due to excess net worth. However, as we noted earlier, VA regulations indicate that assets gifted to someone outside a claimant's household should not be counted as part of net worth if ownership and control of the asset has been relinquished. Also, according to VA officials we spoke with, claims processors do not have access to VA attorneys who could assist them in examining trust agreements and other documents to determine if a claimant has ownership and control of an asset.

Unclear or disparate guidance about counting assets as part of net worth may also lead to different decisions in similar cases. For example, we saw two separate cases in which, just prior to applying, claimants transferred excess assets into trusts to which they did not have access. One of the claims was approved, but the other was denied. For the approved claim, VA determined the claimant did not have ownership and control of the trust and therefore did not count it in the veteran's net worth. For the denied claim, VA also determined that the claimant did not have access to the trust, but the claim was denied because the claims processor felt the applicant was attempting to manipulate assets to qualify for benefits. The denial letter to the claimant explained that VA's income programs are not intended to protect substantial assets or build up the beneficiary's estate for heirs.

Further, we found that VA also lacks specific guidance on how to determine whether or not a claimant's financial resources are sufficient to meet their basic needs without the pension benefit. VA's procedures manual states that pension claims should be denied if a claimant's financial resources are sufficient enough to pay for their living expenses for a "reasonable period of time," but it does not define this term. As a result, claims processors must use their own discretion to determine what period of time is reasonable for claimants to use their assets before needing the assistance of the VA pension. Among case files we reviewed, we found inconsistent claims decisions for claimants whose financial resources would last about the same amount of time and who had similar life expectancies. For example, two veterans whose net worth was projected to provide for their needs for 2 years received different decisions on their claims based on this net worth. In this instance, a 90-year-old with a life expectancy of 4.4 years was denied benefits, while a 94-year-old with a life expectancy of 3.2 years was approved. Also, when we presented a hypothetical scenario of a claimant whose financial resources would last a specific amount of time, different processors at the same PMC gave differing opinions about whether the claimant should be approved for benefits.[27]

Many Organizations Help VA Pension Claimants Transfer Assets to Qualify for Benefits

Over 200 Organizations Market Services to Help Qualify Veterans and Surviving Spouses for VA Pension Benefits

We identified over 200 organizations located throughout the country that market their services to help veterans and surviving spouses qualify for VA pension benefits by transferring or preserving excess assets.[28] These organizations consist primarily of financial planners and attorneys offering products and services such as annuities and the establishment of trusts, to enable potential VA pension claimants with excess assets to meet financial eligibility criteria for VA pension benefits. For example, one organization marketed on its website that it develops financial plans which include various insurance products, and that its specific area of expertise is to help VA pension claimants with hundreds of thousands of dollars in assets obtain approval for these benefits. Also, a law firm we identified marketed transferring excess assets into special trusts to enable VA pension

[27]We asked claims processors at VA's three PMCs whether they would approve or deny a claim involving an applicant with a life expectancy of 10 years whose net worth would be depleted in 5 years.

[28]See appendix I for an explanation of how we identified these organizations.

claimants to qualify for these benefits. These services being marketed and provided by these organizations are legally permissible under program rules because current federal law and regulations allow VA pension claimants to transfer assets and reduce their net worth prior to applying for benefits. (See figure 2 for excerpts from websites of organizations that offer to transfer assets to help claimants qualify for pension benefits.)

Figure 2: Excerpts from Websites of Organizations That Offer to Transfer Assets to Help Claimants Qualify for VA Pension Benefits

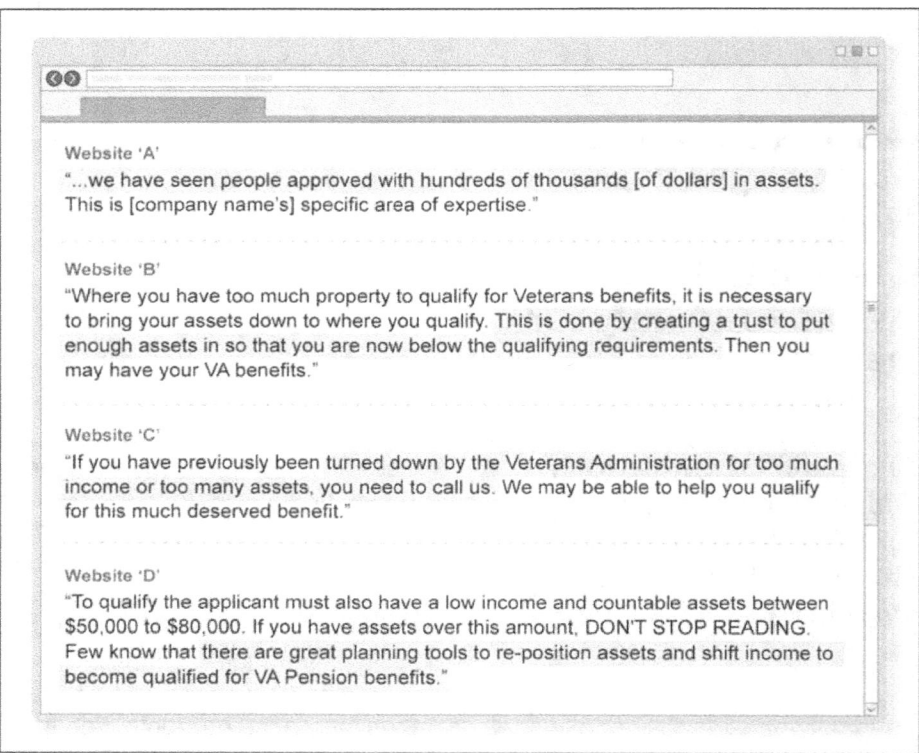

Source: GAO display of excerpts from company websites accessed December 2011 and April 2012.

During our investigative calls to 19 organizations, all of them correctly pointed out that pension claimants can legally transfer assets prior to applying. These organizations indicated that it is possible to qualify for VA pension benefits despite having excess assets, and almost all provided information on how to transfer these assets. (See figure 3 for transcript excerpts of calls with organizations on services they provide to qualify for VA pension benefits.)[29]

Figure 3: Transcript Excerpts of Calls with Organizations Providing Products and Services to Help Claimants Qualify for VA Pension Benefits

A GAO investigator phoned multiple companies on behalf of a fictitious father, who was portrayed as a veteran seeking VA pension benefits, to learn about the services provided by the companies. Below are excerpts from three calls in which a company representative told the investigator that VA beneficiaries may qualify for benefits by transferring assets.

Company representative:

"...I will just tell you this: The VA allows you to qualify, regardless of what your assets are. And **I've had people with over a million dollars qualify for this benefit.**"

Company representative:

"It is a means-tested and an asset-tested benefit, but essentially there are legal work-arounds. And if you know, it's **basically you have to put together a good presentation for the Veterans Administration.** And that's what we do. We help people position assets and coordinate the presentation effort to the VA."

Later in the call:

"Yeah, **I've qualified people with that — beyond $700,000 worth of liquid assets.** So that's not the issue."

Company representative:

"What that means is basically repositioning the assets to where again, the software tells us what we can and can't do. But I'm just going to give you kind of a hypothetical: For example, **you may be able to reposition, reallocate those funds into a trust... And we're allowed to apply for VA benefits the day after,** by reallocating those funds, so that dad can qualify."

For a complete transcript of all three phone calls, see appendix II.

Source: GAO and company representatives.

Note: To hear additional audio excerpts from the three phone calls, go to http://www.gao.gov/multimedia/video#video_id=590696.

A number of different strategies may be used to transfer pension claimants' excess assets so that they meet financial eligibility thresholds. Among the 19 organizations our investigative staff contacted, about half advised transferring excess assets into an irrevocable trust with a family member as the trustee to direct funds to pay for the veteran's expenses. About half

---

[29]Representatives' quotes in figure 3 are not from organizations whose websites are quoted in figure 2.

GAO-12-540 Veterans' Benefits

also advised placing excess assets into some type of annuity. Among these, several advised placing excess assets into an immediate annuity that generates income for the client. In employing this strategy, assets that VA would count when determining financial eligibility for pension benefits are converted into monthly income. This monthly income would fall below program thresholds and enable the claimant to still qualify for the benefits. About one-third of the organizations recommended strategies that included the use of both annuities and trusts. For example, one organization we contacted advised repositioning some excess assets into an irrevocable trust, with the son as the trustee, and placing remaining excess assets into a deferred annuity that would not be completely accessible, since most of the funds could not be withdrawn without a penalty. In addition, several organization representatives we interviewed also told us they may advise using caretaker agreements to enable a client to qualify for VA pension benefits. Organizations told us this strategy generally involves the pension claimant transferring assets to family members as part of a contract, in exchange for caretaker services to be provided by these family members for the remainder of the claimant's lifetime.

Some organization representatives we interviewed told us that transferring assets to qualify for VA pension benefits is advantageous for elderly pension claimants because it enables them to have more income to pay for care expenses and remain out of a nursing home for a longer period of time. For example, representatives from one organization said the use of immediate income annuities allows pension claimants to increase their monthly income that, combined with the VA pension, could help pay for assisted living or in-home care costs. Other financial planners and attorneys said if claimants do not conduct financial or estate planning to qualify for the VA pension and instead spend down their assets prior to applying, the monthly amount of the pension benefit they eventually receive may be insufficient to pay for their long-term care. They said that, as a result, these claimants may decide to seek Medicaid coverage for nursing home care because of their lack of financial resources, when they could have remained in an assisted living facility or at home with the aid of the VA pension. Some of these organizations told us that nursing home care financed by Medicaid is more costly for the government than if the veteran had received the VA pension benefit and obtained care in a lower-cost assisted living facility.

Many organizations we identified also conduct presentations on VA pension benefits at assisted living or retirement communities to identify prospective clients. According to attorneys and officials from state attorneys general offices we spoke with, managers of assisted living facilities or retirement communities may have an interest in inviting organization representatives to conduct presentations on VA pension benefits because these benefits allow them to obtain new residents by making the costs more affordable. For example, we obtained documentation indicating that one retirement community paid an organization representative a fee for a new resident he helped the facility obtain. Another community in another state paid organization representatives fees to assist residents in completing the VA pension application.

Some Products and Services May Adversely Affect Claimants

Some products may not be suitable for elderly veterans because they may lose access to funds they may need for future expenses, such as medical care. To help elderly clients become financially eligible for VA pension benefits, some organizations may sell deferred annuities, which would make the client unable to access the funds in the annuity during their expected lifetime without facing high withdrawal fees, according to some attorneys we spoke with. An elderly advocacy organization representative we spoke with also noted that elderly individuals are impoverishing themselves by purchasing these products when they may need the transferred assets to pay for their long-term care expenses. As part of our investigative work, one organization provided a financial plan to qualify for VA pension benefits that included both an immediate annuity as well as a deferred annuity for an 86-year-old veteran that would generate payments only after the veteran's life expectancy.

Some organizations that assist in transferring assets to qualify people for VA pension benefits may not consider the implications of these transfers on eligibility for Medicaid coverage for long-term care. Individuals who transfer assets to qualify for the VA pension may become ineligible for Medicaid coverage for long-term care services they may need in the future. For example, asset transfers that may enable someone to qualify for the VA pension program, such as gifts to someone not residing in a claimant's household, the purchase of deferred annuities, or the establishment of trusts, may result in a delay in Medicaid eligibility if the assets were transferred for less than fair market value during the 60-month look-back period. According to several attorneys we spoke with, some organization representatives are unaware or indifferent to the adverse effects on Medicaid eligibility of the products and services they market to qualify for the VA pension. As a result, potential pension claimants may be unaware the purchase of these products and services may subsequently delay their eligibility for Medicaid.

In addition to the potential adverse impact of transferring assets, we heard concerns that marketing strategies used by some of these companies may be misleading. According to several attorneys we spoke with, some organization representatives market their services in a way that leads potential pension claimants and their family members to believe they are veterans advocates working for a nonprofit organization, or are endorsed by VA. As a result, they may fail to realize these representatives are actually interested in selling financial Products. For example, some organization representatives may tell attendees during presentations at assisted living facilities that their services consist of providing information on VA pension benefits and assisting with the application, and do not disclose they are insurance agents selling annuities to help people qualify for these benefits. One elder law attorney we spoke with said that many attendees at these presentations may have Alzheimer's disease or dementia, and are not in a position to make decisions about their finances. Therefore, they are vulnerable to being convinced by these representatives that they must purchase a financial product to qualify for these benefits.

Concerns have also been raised that VA's accreditation of individuals to assist with applying for VA benefits may have unintended consequences. According to attorneys and officials in one state, organization representatives use their VA accreditation to assist in preparing claims as a marketing tool that generates trust and allows them to attract clients. Claimants may not understand that this accreditation only means that the individual is proficient in VA's policies and procedures to assist in preparing and submitting VA benefits claims, and does not ensure the Products and services these individuals are selling are in claimant's best interests.

Finally, some organizations may provide erroneous information to clients, or fail to follow through on assisting them with submitting the pension application, which can adversely affect pension claimants. For example, one veteran said he was told by an organization representative to sell his home prior to applying for the VA pension and that he did not have to report the proceeds from the sale on the application. He followed this advice, but VA identified these assets, which caused him to incur a debt to VA of $40,000 resulting from a benefit overpayment. Organizations may also promise assistance with the application process to any interested pension claimant but, unbeknownst to the claimant, may not follow through in providing this service if the claimant does not want to transfer assets. For example, the daughter of a veteran we spoke with, who sought application assistance from an organization representative, told us the representative never submitted her father's pension claim to VA as promised. She learned of this about a year after she thought the claim was submitted and had to reapply through a county veterans service officer. Her father was approved 2 months later but passed away less than a month after his approval. She believes her father could have received benefits for a year if the representative had submitted the claim, and believes he did not do so because she did not want to use his services to transfer assets.

Costs for Services to Transfer Assets Varied, but Some Organizations May Be Charging Prohibited Fees

The costs of services provided by these organizations to assist in qualifying for VA pension benefits varied, but organizations may be charging prohibited fees. Among the 19 organizations our investigative staff contacted for this review, about one-third said they did not charge for their services to help claimants qualify for VA pension benefits. For example, financial planners told us that, generally, there are no direct costs associated with transferring assets into an annuity, but that costs would be included in the terms of the annuity, such as the commission earned by the insurance agent. Among organizations that did charge for services, fees ranged from a few hundred dollars for benefits counseling to up to $10,000 for the establishment of a trust. Also, although federal law prohibits charging fees to assist in completing and submitting applications for VA benefits, representatives from veterans advocacy groups and some attorneys we spoke with raised concerns that these organizations may be charging for fees related to the application, or find ways to circumvent this prohibition, such as by claiming they are charging for benefits counseling. For example, one organization our investigative staff contacted charged $850 to have an attorney work on the application process, a $225 analysis fee, and $1,600 for the establishment of a trust. Another organization representative indicated he charged a "long-term planning fee" of $1,200 to be paid prior to services being provided. The organization representative asked that someone other than the veteran pay this fee, claiming that only disinterested third parties can be charged fees but not the veteran. In addition, concerns have been raised that fees charged may be excessive for the services provided. In July 2011, California enacted a law generally prohibiting unreasonable fees from being charged for these services.[30]

---

[30]See Cal. Civ. Code § 1770(a)(24). An "unreasonable fee" is defined as a fee that is exorbitant and disproportionate to the services performed.

Conclusions

The VA pension program provides a critical benefit to veterans, many of whom are elderly, who have only limited financial resources to support themselves. Current federal law allows veterans to transfer significant assets prior to applying for a VA pension and still be approved for benefits, but this arrangement seems to circumvent the intended purpose of the program and wastes taxpayer dollars. Without stronger controls over asset transfers, similar to other means-tested programs like Medicaid's look-back and penalty period, VA cannot ensure that only those with financial need receive pension benefits. As a result, VA pension claimants who have sufficient assets to pay for their expenses can transfer these assets and qualify for this means-tested benefit. Moreover, because VA's policies and procedures for assessing the initial financial eligibility of pension claimants do not adequately ensure that only veterans and surviving spouses who meet financial eligibility requirements are granted benefits, the program is vulnerable to abuse. In particular, claims processors' reliance on unverified self-reported information when assessing eligibility means that VA cannot be assured that it is obtaining all relevant financial information from claimants, including information on asset transfers, trusts, annuities, and other forms of retirement income. Without all this information, claims processors may improperly grant pension benefits to claimants who do not meet financial eligibility requirements. In addition, while safeguarding fiduciaries' personal information is important, the lack of adequate coordination between VA's pension and fiduciary programs may result in missed opportunities to identify financially ineligible pension claimants, further undermining program integrity. Finally, because VA's guidance concerning when assets should be counted as part of a claimant's net worth and how to evaluate a claimant's net worth in determining eligibility lack sufficient clarity, the program remains vulnerable to inconsistent interpretation and payments to ineligible individuals. Ultimately, in this era of constrained financial resources, VA has a responsibility to manage limited funds wisely, and help ensure continued public support for this important program.

Matter for Congressional Consideration

To ensure that only those in financial need are granted VA pension benefits, Congress should consider establishing a look-back and penalty period for claimants who transfer assets for less than fair market value prior to applying, similar to other means-tested programs.

Recommendations for Executive Action

To improve VA's ability to ensure that only veterans and surviving spouses with financial need receive VA pension benefits, the Secretary of Veterans Affairs should direct the Undersecretary for Benefits to take the following four actions:

1. Modify pension application forms, as well as EVR forms, to include space for claimants or recipients to report asset transfers, and to specify annuities, trusts, or private retirement income. For assets, such as annuities and trusts that are reported, forms should also request related documentation to enable claims processors to determine if claimants or recipients retain ownership and control of these assets.

2. For all claimants, verify financial information during the initial claims assessment process. This may include requesting supporting documentation such as bank statements and tax returns, or using automated databases that can verify financial information.

3. Strengthen coordination between pension and fiduciary programs to identify pension claimants or recipients who have transferred or unreported assets, such as allowing claims processors access to fiduciary field exam reports for these cases.

4. Revise the VA procedures manual to better define the concept of ownership and control to help claims processors determine when specific types of assets such as annuities and trusts should be counted as part of net worth, and establish a more specific criteria for what is considered a reasonable period of time for pension claimants to use up their financial resources before becoming eligible for pension benefits.

Agency Comments and Our Evaluation

We provided a draft of this report to the Secretary of Veterans Affairs for review and comment. In its comments (see app. III), VA generally agreed with our conclusions, concurred with three of our recommendations, and concurred in principle with one other recommendation.

The agency concurred with our recommendation to modify pension application and eligibility verification forms to include a space for claimants or recipients to report asset transfers, to specify annuities, trusts, and private retirement income, and to request related supporting documentation.

VA concurred in principle with our second recommendation that the department verify financial information during the initial claims process. VA noted, however, that conducting this verification would add additional time to adjudicate pension claims. VA said it expects to complete an analysis by November 1, 2012 of whether financial information can be verified without placing undue burdens on claimants and recipients. We acknowledge that rigorous verification processes can sometimes entail additional time during the initial claims phase, but we continue to believe that such verification is an important part of ensuring that VA adequately balances its stewardship responsibilities with its service activities. We support the analysis VA is undertaking.

Regarding our recommendation to strengthen coordination between the pension and fiduciary programs, VA concurred and noted that it has established a workgroup that is developing procedures to further enable fiduciary program staff to share income information with pension program staff.

VA also concurred with our recommendation that the procedures manual be revised to better define the concept of ownership and control of assets and to establish a more specific criteria for what is considered a reasonable period of time for claimants to use their financial resources before becoming eligible for pension benefits. VA stated that it is drafting regulations that would address the effect on eligibility of transferring assets prior to applying for pension benefits. They noted these regulations would address and clarify the various factors VA uses to determine whether a claimant's net worth precludes eligibility for pension benefits and would provide a more consistent set of rules for adjudicating claims. They added that upon completion of the rulemaking proceeding VA will amend its manual provisions consistent with the new regulations and provide the procedures to implement them. They expect to complete this revision by December 1, 2013.

While VA did not directly comment on GAO's Matter for Congressional Consideration related to establishing a statutory look-back and penalty period, VA did note that "unlike Medicaid and SSI, the statutes governing VA's pension program lack provisions addressing the effects of transfers of assets on eligibility for program benefits, e.g., a look-back and penalty period." VA asserted that after identifying gaps in VA's regulations on this point, it has begun drafting regulations to address the issue. VA noted in its comments that any regulations it promulgates on this issue will be subject to challenge in the U.S. Court of Appeals for the Federal Circuit. While we commend VA's efforts in this area, having a clearer statutory basis for this regulatory effort may help ensure that the regulations, should they be finalized, would be more likely to withstand potential legal challenges in the courts.

As agreed with your offices, unless you publicly announce the contents of this report earlier, we plan no further distribution until 30 days from the report date. At that time, we will send copies of this report to the appropriate congressional committees, the Secretary of Veterans Affairs, and other interested parties. The report is also available at no charge on GAO's website at http:/www.gao.gov.

If you or your staff members have any questions concerning this report, please contact me at (202) 512-7215 or bertonid@gao.gov. Contact points for our Offices of Congressional Relations and Public Affairs may be found on the last page of this report. Staff members who made key contributions to this report are listed in appendix IV.

Daniel Bertoni
Director, Education, Workforce,
 and Income Security Issues

Appendix I: Objectives, Scope, and Methodology

The objectives of our review were to examine (1) how the design and management of the Department of Veterans Affairs' (VA) pension program ensure that only those with financial need receive pension benefits and (2) what is known about organizations that are marketing financial products and services to veterans and survivors to enable them to qualify for VA pension benefits.

To determine how the design and management of VA's pension program ensure that only those with financial need receive pension benefits, we reviewed relevant federal laws and regulations, as well as VA's policies, procedures, and guidance regarding how VA assesses financial eligibility for pension benefits. We examined VA's pension application forms and other documents VA uses to collect financial information from pension claimants or recipients. Also, we visited VA's three PMCs in Philadelphia, Milwaukee, and St. Paul, and interviewed staff and officials from these locations as well as from VA's central office. To verify how VA assesses the net worth of pension claimants, we conducted a review of a nongeneralizable random sample of 85 of the total of 3,196 fiscal year 2010 pension claim files completed by each of the PMCs that were entered in VA's electronic case file system, in which VA had to formally determine if the claimant's assets were excessive to be approved for pension benefits. We also reviewed pension claims files VA provided us that involved asset transfers or unreported income and assets. In addition, we reviewed past GAO reports on VA's pension program, Medicaid coverage for long-term care, and the Supplemental Security Income program, as well as relevant federal laws and regulations to learn how these other means-tested programs assess financial eligibility of claimants.

To determine what is known about organizations that are marketing financial products and services to veterans and survivors to enable them to qualify for VA pension benefits, we conducted an Internet search and interviews with stakeholders to identify organizations that market financial products and services to help veterans and surviving spouses meet the eligibility criteria for VA pension benefits. For our Internet search, we used the following search terms "Veterans Affairs and Pension Benefits," "Veterans Affairs and Aid and Attendance Benefits," and "Veterans Affairs and Pension and Aid and Attendance Benefits." We applied three criteria when we examined the content of the websites obtained from our results to develop a list of organizations that market these services. To be included in our list, the organization's website must indicate they provide services to help someone qualify for VA pension benefits or assess eligibility for VA benefits, and either indicate they provide products such as annuities or trusts to transfer assets or indicate they provide services to protect or preserve assets. In addition to our Internet search, we also included in our list several organizations that met these criteria that we identified through interviews with veterans advocacy groups, state officials, and attorneys. In applying these criteria, we developed a list of over 200 organizations that market these services. We used a methodology where two analysts had to agree that the organization met the criteria.

Our investigative staff contacted a judgmental sample of 25 of the organizations on our list posing as the son of an 86-year-old veteran with over $300,000 in countable assets who is interested in applying for VA pension benefits. The 25 organizations were judgmentally selected to achieve geographic dispersion and include both financial planners and attorneys. For these calls, we sought to identify the types of products being marketed, their terms and costs, and the effect on the veterans' access to their assets. The addresses for the main offices of the companies selected represent 13 different states that encompass about one-half of the veteran population age 65 and older. These states also include three states that represent one-fourth of the veteran population age 65 and older. Of the 25 companies contacted, our investigative staff was able to have a discussion with a representative for 19 of these organizations. For the other six companies, we either did not receive a response to a phone message or our phone calls to the organization were not answered.

To learn more about the types of products and services that may be provided to enable someone to meet the financial eligibility criteria for VA pension benefits, we also interviewed attorneys and financial planners, as well as representatives from the National Association of Insurance Commissioners. To identify the implications of transferring assets to qualify for VA pension benefits, we spoke with attorneys, representatives of veterans and elderly advocacy groups, state and local government officials, and family members of pension claimants that we were referred to who used the services of organizations to apply for these benefits. To learn about any investigations involving the practices of some of these companies, we spoke with officials from VA's Office of Inspector General and officials from state attorneys general offices in California, Iowa, Montana, Oregon, Pennsylvania, Texas, and Washington.

We conducted this performance audit from July 2011 to May 2012 in accordance with generally accepted government auditing standards. Those standards require that we plan and perform the audit to obtain sufficient, appropriate evidence to provide a reasonable basis for our findings and conclusions based on our audit objectives. We believe that the evidence obtained provides a reasonable basis for our findings and conclusions based on our audit objectives.

Appendix II: Full Transcript of Selected Calls with Organizations Providing Products and Services to Help Claimants Qualify for VA Pension Benefits

The Department of Veterans Affairs (VA) provides pension benefits to eligible veterans and surviving spouses whose income and assets are below program thresholds. However, current VA regulations permit claimants to transfer excess assets prior to applying. Organizations market financial Products and services to help prospective pension claimants transfer excess assets and become financially eligible for these benefits. An investigator from our Forensic Audits and Investigative Service team had phone conversations with representatives from 19 of these organizations to learn if the organization would transfer a claimant's excess assets, the types of services provided, and any fees charged. (See appendix I for more information on our scope and methodology.) Because VA's pension benefits are meant for claimants with financial need, we selected portions of three of these calls that show organizations transfer significant assets to help claimants qualify for the benefits, and the types of services they provide to do so. The full transcripts of these three calls are provided below.

Call 1: Caller is a GAO investigator phoning on behalf of his fictitious 86-year-old father who was a veteran, seeking VA pension benefits, who wants to learn about the services provided by the company. The company representative describes how his father can qualify for these benefits, despite having significant assets.

(Whereupon, an outgoing call was placed by the GAO investigator to a company representative.)

COMPANY REPRESENTATIVE: [name].

GAO INVESTIGATOR: Hello?

COMPANY REPRESENTATIVE: Hello, this is [name].

GAO INVESTIGATOR: Hey, [name], this is [name].

COMPANY REPRESENTATIVE: Hey, [name], how are you doing?

GAO INVESTIGATOR: I'm doing good. I got your messages. I'm sorry, it's just been a little nuts.

COMPANY REPRESENTATIVE: Not a problem.

GAO INVESTIGATOR: You still there?

COMPANY REPRESENTATIVE: Yeah, I'm here. Yes.

Appendix II: Full Transcript of Selected Calls
with Organizations Providing Products and
Services to Help Claimants Qualify for VA
Pension Benefits

GAO INVESTIGATOR: I was calling — it's your brother or your brother-in-law that I spoke to?

COMPANY REPRESENTATIVE: My brother-in-law.

GAO INVESTIGATOR: Yeah, I'm trying to make a decision here with my father. We are going to have to, you know, make some decisions on what we're going to do with him. And I just wanted to see, you know, before we go draining all his resources, what our options are.

COMPANY REPRESENTATIVE: Okay. You don't — he's not in a community yet or he is?

GAO INVESTIGATOR: He's not, he's still living at his house.

COMPANY REPRESENTATIVE: Okay.

GAO INVESTIGATOR: But, you know, he's got a lot of, you know, physical limitations, he's got difficulty hearing, and he can't really move around, so you know –

COMPANY REPRESENTATIVE: Did his doctor say he needs assistance from another person on a regular basis?

GAO INVESTIGATOR: Well, I imagine. I mean, I didn't ask that question, specifically, but I'm sure he would. I mean, right now, you know, we're kind of trying to take care of him ourselves, and you know, we've got somebody helping, but we're going to need something more full time.

COMPANY REPRESENTATIVE: Yeah. You guys are helping out with cooking, cleaning. Is he still able to drive or no?

GAO INVESTIGATOR: No.

COMPANY REPRESENTATIVE: Okay. So he needs transportation. You know, these are the things they are looking for. Did you say his vision is an issue?

GAO INVESTIGATOR: No, his hearing, is what I said.

COMPANY REPRESENTATIVE: (Laughter) I'm sorry.

GAO INVESTIGATOR: And his, not yours.

COMPANY REPRESENTATIVE: (Laughter) Well, maybe mine, a little bit. Anyhow, yeah, the VA kind of looks at, you know, daily activities — the activities of daily living. And if he can't do some of those things, he needs assistance, you know, then he can qualify for the benefit.

They don't mean if somebody is completely bedridden or handicapped, they just mean if somebody needs assistance and help with some parts of their life.

Appendix II: Full Transcript of Selected Calls
with Organizations Providing Products and
Services to Help Claimants Qualify for VA
Pension Benefits

What we would be able to do – we have people that are still able to drive and live at home, but they can't do certain — they can't carry the bags from the car if they go grocery shopping, because they don't have the dexterity or the strength.

GAO INVESTIGATOR: All right.

COMPANY REPRESENTATIVE: So, you know, the VA looks at it and says, they can't even go shopping for themselves, they can't carry the bags from the car, they can't lift them, you know, how are they going to get them into the house?

GAO INVESTIGATOR: Well, I'm sure that's not a problem. I mean, he definitely is, you know, he needs help with just going to the bathroom, getting in and out of bed and stuff like that.

COMPANY REPRESENTATIVE: Yeah. He needs help getting in and out of bed, getting to the bathroom, those are the things they're looking at. Absolutely, he needs this assistance, and he can qualify for the benefit.

And everything else is just about preparing yourself for the benefit, doing the paperwork and so forth.

GAO INVESTIGATOR: Okay.

COMPANY REPRESENTATIVE: And that a process, in and of itself. What I would suggest is get together, you know. This is — this doesn't— this isn't like a one-time sit-down and it's all done, you know. This can take several weeks, and sometimes even up to six weeks, to get all the paperwork completed.

GAO INVESTIGATOR: Okay.

COMPANY REPRESENTATIVE: So you know, but it's a matter of getting started. You know, and that's what I — you know, if your dad needs assistance, and he was a wartime Veteran, we can get him the benefit. All right?

GAO INVESTIGATOR: Okay. Well, you know what, my big concern – [inaudible] yeah, you know, which I mentioned to your brother-in-law is, um — you know, he's got some assets, and I don't know how that affects things.

COMPANY REPRESENTATIVE: You know, the assets come into play, and that's part of the process. We would explain all that to you – what, what — where you need to go, how — what needs to be done.

Ideally, an accredited attorney that we – that we work with, he'll have that conversation with you. He'll explain that to you in more detail.

GAO INVESTIGATOR: Okay.

COMPANY REPRESENTATIVE: But anyone — and I will just tell you this. The VA allows you to qualify, regardless of what your assets are. And I've had people with over a million dollars qualify for this benefit.

Appendix II: Full Transcript of Selected Calls
with Organizations Providing Products and
Services to Help Claimants Qualify for VA
Pension Benefits

GAO INVESTIGATOR: Wow.

COMPANY REPRESENTATIVE: So you know, you'll hear you can only have this much money, you can do this. You'll even be told you don't qualify.

GAO INVESTIGATOR: And how do you do that, though, I mean, that's what I don't understand.

COMPANY REPRESENTATIVE: Well, you have to reposition the assets, that's all. You know, like I said, that's — that's part of what the attorney will talk about.

From a process standpoint, I'll gather all the information that we need from you, what will go on the VA application. And we will get a letter back from our VA-accredited attorney, and he will outline and tell you you do or you don't qualify.

Some people qualify immediately; other people, like in your situation, if your family has some assets, you may have to jump through some hoops in order to get the benefit.

But the VA outlines it and says, this is what you're allowed to do, in order to qualify.

And, you know, we'll share that with you. We'll show you exactly what you need to do, how to do it, because it has to be done a certain way in order to qualify.

Look at this as kind of something you're going to do one time, all right? This isn't like doing your taxes, you know, where you need to remember it to understand it for next year.

You are going to do this once, and it's going to be out of your life.

GAO INVESTIGATOR: Okay. Here's a question that I have. Does he still have control of the assets?

COMPANY REPRESENTATIVE: Your family will.

GAO INVESTIGATOR: Okay.

COMPANY REPRESENTATIVE: Yeah, your family will. I mean, all his money, his monthly money, will go right into his checking account, just like it probably does, Social Security, pension, whatever. The VA benefit will go right into his checking account. All that money will keep going right into his account, and he will have access to that.

GAO INVESTIGATOR: Okay, all right. Okay, just so I understand it, so you're just talking about putting it under a different name or are you putting it in a special account?

COMPANY REPRESENTATIVE: [name], here's the thing. I can't get into all that with you over the phone.

GAO INVESTIGATOR: Okay.

COMPANY REPRESENTATIVE: It will get so complicated and so confusing. This conversation that I need to have with you will take about an hour, just to get the process started, and then we will get into all that stuff.

Every person I have tried to help with this benefit, when they try to get to the — like into the high school level questions, before understanding the kindergarten and grade school level questions, they never get the benefit, because they can't — they can't under —they get so confused.

So it's almost like, once you've seen a dead body you can't unsee it, and you can't focus on anything else. And so what I'm trying to share with you, you know, if you just, you know, take a bite at a time, you know, like the old saying, you can't eat an elephant in one bite, we need just a bite of your time.

You will get through this and you'll get the money.

But if we try to jump ahead, you know, I'll tell you, it's never been successful.

GAO INVESTIGATOR: Okay. What –

COMPANY REPRESENTATIVE: And I hope you understand. I'm just giving you my expertise and experience in this.

We do over — we submit over four hundred apps a month, and everybody gets the benefit, so we know how to do it, we know how to get it done.

And nothing is going to be a surprise to you. Everything is going to be here, this is your option. If you want this, you've got to do this.

And then it's up for you to decide. But it's just a matter of getting you to that point where you have all the facts, so you can make a decision.

And so the questions you're asking are all valid, you know, they are all the questions that we'll be delving into very deeply. If you need a CPA involved, we have a CPA on our team. We have our attorney on our team that I use, [name]. He'll be a part of all the conversations if we need, so all throughout.

And none of that is costing you any money, because that's part of my fee.

But what I'm saying is, all those questions that you have now, when you are ready for the answers, we'll have those conversations. But right now, you're not ready for the answers. It's difficult to understand this, why this, what that?

All those answers you are going to get from me right now are going to create more and more questions, and things are going to get so confusing for you.

GAO INVESTIGATOR: Okay.

**Appendix II: Full Transcript of Selected Calls
with Organizations Providing Products and
Services to Help Claimants Qualify for VA
Pension Benefits**

COMPANY REPRESENTATIVE: This process is already confusing enough, I've got to tell you.

GAO INVESTIGATOR: Okay.

COMPANY REPRESENTATIVE: There are some three hundred to four hundred thousand applications a month — I mean, I shouldn't say a month. The VA has over — between three hundred and four hundred thousand applications backlogged, sitting there, because people didn't do the process right, and it will take them up to two years to get approved.

You know, that — that's — it is difficult. It has to be done a certain way, and I'll get you there. I promise, I'll get you there, but you just have to go through it step-by-step.

GAO INVESTIGATOR: Okay. Well, the only other question I have then is the cost. What is the cost involved?

COMPANY REPRESENTATIVE: If there is any cost, it would be with the attorney. They charge — they'll charge a fee for setting up certain documents, and we'll get to that, as well.

The worst case, let's say your dad, he has a house, and you're not able to sell the house. See, while he's living in it, they don't care that he owns a home, but when he's out of the house, they consider it an asset.

We have to — we'll have to do something with the house, as well. If you were planning on selling it, fine.

If you weren't planning on selling it, that's fine, too, but we'll have to address it.

The worst case scenario would be about fourteen hundred bucks. That's a worst case scenario.

GAO INVESTIGATOR: Okay.

COMPANY REPRESENTATIVE: And when you understand what that all entails, you'll be like, geez, fourteen hundred bucks, let's find out tomorrow. That's another thing, you know, when you understand everything that you get with that.

And he'll make sure everything is done the right way so that the VA can never come back at you, seeing that the house is protected, your mother is protected, you know.

I'm just saying, there's a whole lot to it, and to try to answer it over the phone is more than tough.

GAO INVESTIGATOR: Okay. All right. So there's no — that's just an attorney fee? I mean, there's no fee for you?

COMPANY REPRESENTATIVE: Exactly.

Appendix II: Full Transcript of Selected Calls
with Organizations Providing Products and
Services to Help Claimants Qualify for VA
Pension Benefits

GAO INVESTIGATOR: There's no fee for you, at all?

COMPANY REPRESENTATIVE: No, not at all.

GAO INVESTIGATOR: Does the VA pay you or something?

COMPANY REPRESENTATIVE: Hang on a second. Let me do this. I hate to try to get you — are you busy during the day?

GAO INVESTIGATOR: Ummmm.

COMPANY REPRESENTATIVE: Is there like an hour of time that you and I can get together and get the process started, so I can show you how — how it all works?

GAO INVESTIGATOR: Yeah, I mean, probably, but probably not until, you know, after the holidays.

COMPANY REPRESENTATIVE: Okay. Then let's do this. If you have your schedule, my schedule is tied up until the second week of January, already filled with seminars and things to — so people can come and see me. The second week I have at least two seminars, and I usually have thirty to forty people at each seminar.

GAO INVESTIGATOR: Uh-huh.

COMPANY REPRESENTATIVE: And then about half of those people sit down with me and want to go to the next step.

GAO INVESTIGATOR: Right.

COMPANY REPRESENTATIVE: So if I do two or four presentations, I mean, I've got thirty to fifty appointments during the second week of January. So if you and I can get together in the first week, I can get you started before all that mess starts.

GAO INVESTIGATOR: Okay. Well, I wonder if it wouldn't be beneficial to go to one of the seminars?

COMPANY REPRESENTATIVE: Well, the seminar is in [name].

GAO INVESTIGATOR: In where?

COMPANY REPRESENTATIVE: In [name], but really, what I do there is more of a blanket meeting.

If you already know you have a situation, you already know you have an interest, I go over that same information that I go over in the seminar. But the seminar, it's just information, and I will be giving that to you face-to-face, and be able to collect the information and get started on the process.

Appendix II: Full Transcript of Selected Calls
with Organizations Providing Products and
Services to Help Claimants Qualify for VA
Pension Benefits

GAO INVESTIGATOR: Okay. Yeah, I mean, I don't have a lot of questions, you know, I just want to know what types of Products : you're talking about that we would — where the assets would go, how — I mean, are we talking about –

COMPANY REPRESENTATIVE: It all depends on your dad's needs. Right now we don't know – I don't know anything about your situation. I don't know what your costs are, I don't know what his expenses, his needs are. I don't have any idea what the cash flow management requirements will be –

GAO INVESTIGATOR: Yeah.

COMPANY REPRESENTATIVE: — this year, next year, five years down the road. You know, as a financial advisor, you know, I come from the banking industry, where I worked in the trust department, and my clients were all multi, multi-millionaires. And all I did for them was identify what their needs were going to be year in and year out, into the future –

GAO INVESTIGATOR: Right.

COMPANY REPRESENTATIVE: — protecting their assets, so that they knew that money was going to be there (unintelligible). Like your dad, the last thing he wants to do is have his nest egg at risk.

GAO INVESTIGATOR: Right.

COMPANY REPRESENTATIVE: He's going to need — he's going to need income from it to maybe offset some of the cost of his retirement community, perhaps.

GAO INVESTIGATOR: Uh-huh.

COMPANY REPRESENTATIVE: I don't know, you know, I don't have any answers, at this point, because I don't know what his needs are, what your family needs are, you know, how many kids are there, who all is involved.

GAO INVESTIGATOR: I mean, basically, it's just him. I mean, he's got his Social Security, and then, if he qualifies for the VA Pension, he would have that. So I imagine that would be enough income for him. So it's just a matter of doing something with the assets, so he doesn't lose it. So –

COMPANY REPRESENTATIVE: Exactly. And that's something you and I will discuss and work on. Are you — are you handling his affairs now?

GAO INVESTIGATOR: Yeah, uh-huh.

COMPANY REPRESENTATIVE: So you take care of all of his bills?

GAO INVESTIGATOR: Yeah.

COMPANY REPRESENTATIVE: So you are the person who understands best, you know, what your parents, you know, what the family, you know, your father, your mother, your parents, what their requirements are.

Now your mother has passed; is that correct?

GAO INVESTIGATOR: Yes, uh-huh.

COMPANY REPRESENTATIVE: Okay, so we're just talking about your dad here.

GAO INVESTIGATOR: Right.

COMPANY REPRESENTATIVE: So here's — the VA just increased the payment to the Veteran, single Veteran, to right around seventeen hundred a month, tax-free, so it's a pretty substantial benefit; that's over twenty thousand dollars a year.

If you are looking at his — looking at what his Social Security is –

GAO INVESTIGATOR: Right.

COMPANY REPRESENTATIVE: — you add that, plus his VA, it may cover his long-term care facility.

GAO INVESTIGATOR: Uh-huh, yeah, his Social Security is twelve hundred, so you're talking about somewhere close to almost three thousand dollars a month.

COMPANY REPRESENTATIVE: Yeah, exactly, so that's not bad, that's not bad. Now it depends on what kind of community he would be looking at, but you know, that's. .

You know, the hardest part is getting started, and then once you get to a certain point, you'll be like, yeah, I get it, I get it, now I understand, this is what we do.

Let me ask you, is Tuesday the 3rd or is Wednesday the 4th a better day for you?

GAO INVESTIGATOR: Well, probably Wednesday will be better for me.

COMPANY REPRESENTATIVE: And you're in [state]?

GAO INVESTIGATOR: Yes.

COMPANY REPRESENTATIVE: Okay. How does 10 a.m. work?

GAO INVESTIGATOR: Are you talking about coming down to me or where?

COMPANY REPRESENTATIVE: Yeah, absolutely, I'd come to you.

Appendix II: Full Transcript of Selected Calls
with Organizations Providing Products and
Services to Help Claimants Qualify for VA
Pension Benefits

GAO INVESTIGATOR: That sounds good, tentatively. I've got to check and make sure that — I have to check a couple things here, but I mean, it sounds good.

COMPANY REPRESENTATIVE: What address is the best place to meet you?

GAO INVESTIGATOR: Well, you know, I'm guessing that it might be just as good to do it at the office. I'll tell you what, are you going to be around this afternoon?

COMPANY REPRESENTATIVE: Yeah, do you want to give me a call back?

GAO INVESTIGATOR: Yeah, let me give you a call back. Let me check the schedule and make sure it's good. I think it would probably be easier just to do this at the office.

COMPANY REPRESENTATIVE: Okay. What city is it?

GAO INVESTIGATOR: I'm sorry?

COMPANY REPRESENTATIVE: What city is your office in?

GAO INVESTIGATOR: In [city].

COMPANY REPRESENTATIVE: That sounds so familiar. As you are going down 83, that's

GAO INVESTIGATOR: Near [city].

COMPANY REPRESENTATIVE: Near [city], okay, (unintelligible). All right, good. Give me a call back just to confirm if 10 a.m. works. If I don't answer, just leave a message. I may go out and do some shopping (unintelligible).

GAO INVESTIGATOR: All right. I'll just leave a message on your voicemail.

COMPANY REPRESENTATIVE: Yeah, and — good.

GAO INVESTIGATOR: Sounds good.

COMPANY REPRESENTATIVE: All right, [name].

GAO INVESTIGATOR: Thanks for your time, I appreciate it.

COMPANY REPRESENTATIVE: Nice talking to you.

GAO INVESTIGATOR: Alright, Bye.

Appendix II: Full Transcript of Selected Calls
with Organizations Providing Products and
Services to Help Claimants Qualify for VA
Pension Benefits

Call 2: Caller is a GAO investigator phoning on behalf of his fictitious 86-year-old father who was a veteran, seeking VA pension benefits, who wants to learn about the services provided by the company. The company representative describes how his father can qualify for these benefits, despite having significant assets.

(Whereupon, an outgoing call was placed by the GAO investigator to a company representative.)

COMPANY REPRESENTATIVE: Hello? Hello?

GAO INVESTIGATOR: Hi.

COMPANY REPRESENTATIVE: Hi. This is [name]. Did somebody call this number?

GAO INVESTIGATOR: Yeah, I did. I did. I was trying to get some information on VA benefits.

COMPANY REPRESENTATIVE: Okay. What can I help you with?

GAO INVESTIGATOR: Well, I'm just trying to figure out my — this is for my father.

COMPANY REPRESENTATIVE: Uh-huh.

GAO INVESTIGATOR: And, you know, he's not currently getting benefits. He gets Social Security.

COMPANY REPRESENTATIVE: Right.

GAO INVESTIGATOR: But, you know, I was — I'm trying to see if maybe he could qualify for benefits. But the problem is he's got, you know, some assets, and I'm not sure, you know, if that precludes him from getting benefits or not. So I wanted to talk to somebody –

COMPANY REPRESENTATIVE: No. No. Is he — does he need some help around the house or has he got some medical or physical impairments –

GAO INVESTIGATOR: Yeah.

COMPANY REPRESENTATIVE: — right now?

GAO INVESTIGATOR: Yeah. I mean, he's 86. I mean, mentally he's fine. But, you know, physically he needs a lot of help in just, you know, walking and getting in and out of bed.

COMPANY REPRESENTATIVE: Okay.

**Appendix II: Full Transcript of Selected Calls
with Organizations Providing Products and
Services to Help Claimants Qualify for VA
Pension Benefits**

GAO INVESTIGATOR: And, I mean, yeah, he needs help.

COMPANY REPRESENTATIVE: Sure. If you will — if you will do me a favor, I'm going to send you — do you have an e-mail address?

GAO INVESTIGATOR: Well, not really. But, I mean, I can probably get something. But what do you need?

COMPANY REPRESENTATIVE: Well, I was going to send you a little form, and if you can just spend a few minutes and fill it out, then I can tell you if your father is available for benefits or not.

GAO INVESTIGATOR: Okay. I mean, I mean, basically I'm assuming he –

COMPANY REPRESENTATIVE: I probably could do this — I could do this over the phone, too. But right now I'm just going and jumping on a conference call. So I can call you back and I can ask you the questions I need to ask you, if you want. Maybe in — I'd say within a couple of hours I can get back with you.

GAO INVESTIGATOR: Okay. Yeah, that might work.

COMPANY REPRESENTATIVE: Okay. It is a means-tested and an asset-tested – uh, benefit, but – um, essentially there are legal work-arounds. And if you know, it's basically you have to put together a good presentation for the Veterans Administration. And that's what we do. We help people um — position assets and coordinate the presentation effort to the VA. So there's really not many kinds — if, in fact, your father has lost some of the activities of daily living, then we really can't get him qualified. So I'll just –

GAO INVESTIGATOR: Yeah.

COMPANY REPRESENTATIVE: — make a short explanation like that.

GAO INVESTIGATOR: Yeah. And just to kind of make it short, I mean, his income isn't the thing, because he's only getting Social Security. But he's got assets that are probably — between his house and some savings and stuff, he's probably, you know, a little bit over $500,000.

And I'm wondering if that precludes him from qualifying.

COMPANY REPRESENTATIVE: No. No, it doesn't, especially if he's got a little bit of uh — flexibility. How much is the house worth? The house is really not an issue at all.

GAO INVESTIGATOR: Yeah, that's probably about 200,000.

COMPANY REPRESENTATIVE: Oh, so you have 300 in other stuff? Okay. Yeah, I've qualified people with that — beyond $700,000 worth of liquid assets. So that's not the issue. But sometimes the older folks, you know, your father being 82 –

GAO INVESTIGATOR: Eighty-six.

Appendix II: Full Transcript of Selected Calls
with Organizations Providing Products and
Services to Help Claimants Qualify for VA
Pension Benefits

COMPANY REPRESENTATIVE: Eighty-six, I'm sorry. Sometimes they — oh, they're not — what would be the word? They're sometimes control freaks, meaning sometimes what we have to do is retitle assets. He would still be totally in control of them, but not under his direct purvey.

So if he can understand the strategy, he could understand that, you know, he's entitled to the benefit. It could be — he's single right now?

GAO INVESTIGATOR: Yeah, yeah. His wife is dead.

COMPANY REPRESENTATIVE: Okay. So, you know, basically he performed for his country. If he was able to get aid and attendance, he would get real close to — actually, this year is $19,736 per year. And if that means something to him, then we can help him out. If it doesn't, then

he'll just have to go through spend-down and spend it.

So we can — we can make it work, but he's got to be willing to help us. Okay? We can't force people to do something that they're not wanting to do.

GAO INVESTIGATOR: I got it.

COMPANY REPRESENTATIVE: Okay. It's real simple –

GAO INVESTIGATOR: What sorts of things are you talking about? I mean, where do we put it?

COMPANY REPRESENTATIVE: Well, for instance, do you have power of attorney for him right now?

GAO INVESTIGATOR: Well, I don't. But, you know, he's pretty — he's pretty lucid. I mean, I — I can probably get it.

COMPANY REPRESENTATIVE: Well, typically speaking, for people that have had a child or relative assigned a power of attorney, then they've kind of realized that, you know, if something happens, they may need some help. Somebody acting in their financial capacity if they get in a situation where they can't perform or somebody to make some medical decisions for them.

So at that point in time, they've kind of acquiesced to the fact that, you know, at this point in my life, I need a little bit of help.

So I was going to say, if he'd already given you power of attorney, then essentially what he said is, you know, he trusts you.

GAO INVESTIGATOR: Uh-huh.

COMPANY REPRESENTATIVE: And if that's the case, then essentially it's going to be that type of a relationship where things may be put into special types of trusts where

Appendix II: Full Transcript of Selected Calls
with Organizations Providing Products and
Services to Help Claimants Qualify for VA
Pension Benefits

he is still — where you would have a fiduciary responsibility to him. So it's a contractual obligation. It's — all the money is for the benefit of him, but it's not under his direct control.

Now, that's not necessarily the only way it can be done. There are also what we call care contracts where essentially he can kind of prepay in a contractual manner for his future care. It gets it out of his immediate possession and would help qualify for those types of benefits.

So there's a myriad of strategies. I work with an attorney. We'll make sure it works for you. But he just has to understand that either he wants to get the benefit or he doesn't. If he does, we can make it work. If he doesn't, then that's okay, too.

GAO INVESTIGATOR: Right. Well, I mean –

COMPANY REPRESENTATIVE: It's up to him.

GAO INVESTIGATOR: — I don't think he wants to lose his assets. And, you know, you know, we don't want him to lose his assets. And that's — that's the biggest concern now.

COMPANY REPRESENTATIVE: Right. There's — there's a — yeah, well, he will if he needs the care. Then the other issue you have coming up, too, of course, is sometimes folks that mostly qualify for the benefit will essentially possibly qualify for Medicaid, too. And what that means is that, yes, I mean, if his expenses go to $6-7-8-9-10,000 a month, then he will lose his assets unless he does something to protect them. So we can help out in that regard, too.

GAO INVESTIGATOR: Okay.

COMPANY REPRESENTATIVE: It's — you really don't have — you don't have an e-mail address really?

GAO INVESTIGATOR: Well, I can get one for you, yeah. I'm not real computer — I'm not a computer guy. That's all.

COMPANY REPRESENTATIVE: Okay. Well, I can appreciate that. We probably — I'm thinking here — is this your cell number?

GAO INVESTIGATOR: Uh-huh. Uh-huh.

COMPANY REPRESENTATIVE: You wouldn't be able to print it if I gave it to you so –

GAO INVESTIGATOR: Do you have something on your web site?

COMPANY REPRESENTATIVE: I don't have a — I don't have the form embedded. Let's just talk in a couple of hours. I'll ask you the question. You know, I can tell pretty much right now that I can help you out. It's just a matter to the extent where you need to ask your father — well, probably before you talk to me again. Say, Hey, Dad, you know, I talked to an accredited VA application guy, and he says that, you know, we can

**Appendix II: Full Transcript of Selected Calls
with Organizations Providing Products and
Services to Help Claimants Qualify for VA
Pension Benefits**

get you the benefit but there is some strategy involved. And if you want to hear it, fine. If not, that's okay, too.

You know, that's just really what you need to do with this.

GAO INVESTIGATOR: All right. What do you guys charge for that?

COMPANY REPRESENTATIVE: Well, for the — there's two ways. Let's just leave it at a thousand — $1,050, okay?

GAO INVESTIGATOR: Just a straight fee?

COMPANY REPRESENTATIVE: Yeah, $1,050. Of course, what we really want to do is to be able to – we can give you the recommendations and turn you loose, and you go out there on the street and try to implement it.

But, you know, you probably really want to kind of go through us and let us help you in the full way. I will send you enough information and the attorney's information so that you'll understand that we really are a full-fledged service organization and can really help you through this mix.

And then, you know, once we help you out, you can either go down to the local VA office and have them fill out the paperwork. Is your father — is your father in the same town as you or is he — where is your father?

GAO INVESTIGATOR: Yeah, he's not that far away. About, you know, seven, eight miles away.

COMPANY REPRESENTATIVE: Okay. Where — where are you located?

GAO INVESTIGATOR: I'm actually in north [state].

COMPANY REPRESENTATIVE: Oh, are you? What part?

GAO INVESTIGATOR: Well, are you familiar with [city] at all?

COMPANY REPRESENTATIVE: Yes. I went to [college] so –

GAO INVESTIGATOR: Oh, no kidding.

COMPANY REPRESENTATIVE: Yeah. And my sister lives in [city] right now, actually.

GAO INVESTIGATOR: Okay.

COMPANY REPRESENTATIVE: And actually we lived in [city] for a few years when I was real young. Yeah, I'm familiar with [state]. I'm a native of [state]. So, yeah, we can help out. So I wish you had some kind of an e-mail.

Appendix II: Full Transcript of Selected Calls
with Organizations Providing Products and
Services to Help Claimants Qualify for VA
Pension Benefits

GAO INVESTIGATOR: Well, let me see if I can do something. I mean, you know, my brother might have something that I can — I can use.

COMPANY REPRESENTATIVE: Okay. Yeah, because, really, this is a family discussion. You know, all the kids — how many kids are there besides you?

GAO INVESTIGATOR: Just me and my brother.

COMPANY REPRESENTATIVE: All right. So you guys are really going to need to put your heads together and say, hey, this makes sense for us or it doesn't. You know, dad is going to have to cooperate or he's not. And, you know, sometimes, to be honest with you — I deal with older folks, you know — they just don't give a rat's fanny. And so you can't make the horse drink, you know.

GAO INVESTIGATOR: I don't think –

COMPANY REPRESENTATIVE: But if he wants to protect his asset –

GAO INVESTIGATOR: Yeah, I mean, he's — you know, mentally he's fine. I don't think that's going to be a problem. I mean, he –

COMPANY REPRESENTATIVE: All right. Well, if he wants to protect his assets –

GAO INVESTIGATOR: Right.

COMPANY REPRESENTATIVE: Most of the time — most of the time they want their kids to wind up with the money. And sometimes, you know, they don't care as much. But I can't get in your father's head, so you need to kind of ask him if that's the case. If he wants to protect the money, you can have him protect the money.

GAO INVESTIGATOR: Okay. All right.

COMPANY REPRESENTATIVE: Okay?

GAO INVESTIGATOR: Sounds good. All right. I appreciate it. Well, let me see if I can get an e-mail address and give you a buzz back.

COMPANY REPRESENTATIVE: All right. Hey, let me do this. Let me give you my cell number, please, so you should be — because I'm in and out so much. It's [telephone number] –

GAO INVESTIGATOR: Uh-huh.

COMPANY REPRESENTATIVE: — [telephone number].

GAO INVESTIGATOR: Okay.

COMPANY REPRESENTATIVE: [telephone number].

GAO INVESTIGATOR: Okay. All right. Got it.

Appendix II: Full Transcript of Selected Calls
with Organizations Providing Products and
Services to Help Claimants Qualify for VA
Pension Benefits

COMPANY REPRESENTATIVE: All right, buddy. Take care.

GAO INVESTIGATOR: I'm sorry. What did you say your name — what did you say your name was again? I'm sorry.

COMPANY REPRESENTATIVE: [name]—

GAO INVESTIGATOR: [name]. Oh, that's right,[name].

COMPANY REPRESENTATIVE: [name], [name]. Yeah. All right.

GAO INVESTIGATOR: Okay. Thank you.

COMPANY REPRESENTATIVE: Okay. Thank you. Bye now.

Call 3: Caller is a GAO investigator phoning on behalf of his fictitious 86-year-old father who was a veteran, seeking VA pension benefits, who wants to learn about the services provided by the company. The company representative describes how his father can qualify for these benefits, despite having significant assets.

(Whereupon, an outgoing call was placed by the GAO investigator to a company representative.)

SPEAKER ONE: [company name], [name], can I help you?

GAO INVESTIGATOR: Yeah, I hope so. I want to talk to somebody about possibly getting VA benefits for my father.

COMPANY REPRESENTATIVE: Okay. And your name?

GAO INVESTIGATOR: My name is [name].

COMPANY REPRESENTATIVE: Hi, [name]. Can you tell me a little bit about your dad's situation?

GAO INVESTIGATOR: Well, he's a World War II veteran.

COMPANY REPRESENTATIVE: Okay.

GAO INVESTIGATOR: He's 86 years old. Are you there?

COMPANY REPRESENTATIVE: What is the nature of his illness?

GAO INVESTIGATOR: I'm sorry?

COMPANY REPRESENTATIVE: Can you tell me about his illness, please.

GAO INVESTIGATOR: Well, you know, aside from getting old?

Appendix II: Full Transcript of Selected Calls
with Organizations Providing Products and
Services to Help Claimants Qualify for VA
Pension Benefits

COMPANY REPRESENTATIVE: Yeah.

GAO INVESTIGATOR: He's having a lot of — he can't walk too well.

He's got a lot of, you know, joint problems and stuff like that.

So he can't — he needs a lot of help getting in and out of bed, taking baths and stuff like that.

He's also got — he doesn't hear very well.

COMPANY REPRESENTATIVE: And how old is your dad?

GAO INVESTIGATOR: He's 86.

COMPANY REPRESENTATIVE: God bless him.

GAO INVESTIGATOR: I mean, mentally he's fine, but physically he's, you know, I guess just wearing out.

COMPANY REPRESENTATIVE: Where does he live? Is he living with you or is he in a facility?

GAO INVESTIGATOR: No, he's got a place, he's got a house.

COMPANY REPRESENTATIVE: Ok. Are you planning on leaving him at the house, staying at the house?

Is he going to have any in-home health care coming in?

GAO INVESTIGATOR: Yeah, I mean, in-home, I would think, because I mean, mentally he's fine.

COMPANY REPRESENTATIVE: Have you checked with an in-home health care agency to come to the house?

GAO INVESTIGATOR: Well, yeah, he's got people coming in already.

COMPANY REPRESENTATIVE: He does. Okay.

GAO INVESTIGATOR: I mean, that's kind of why I'm –

COMPANY REPRESENTATIVE: I see. The reason why I ask those questions is that in order to get VA benefits, called Aid and Attendance, which is a benefit that the government will pay up to nineteen fifty per month, tax-free, and the government usually pays that 9 months out from the time we apply.

And you get also a retroactive, so it would be 8 months on top of that.

GAO INVESTIGATOR: Okay.

Appendix II: Full Transcript of Selected Calls
with Organizations Providing Products and
Services to Help Claimants Qualify for VA
Pension Benefits

COMPANY REPRESENTATIVE: It's that they need to have something in place like in-home health care already being used or about to be used, or he lives in an assisted-living facility or a nursing home.

And those are key. One of those three things have to be in place or about to be in place.

GAO INVESTIGATOR: He is getting help already at the house. I mean, that's one of the things.

I mean, we're spending a lot of money.

And you know, he's got — he's got some assets, but I mean, as far as income, all he's got is his Social Security.

COMPANY REPRESENTATIVE: Tell me about his Social Security. What is coming in per month, as far as income?

GAO INVESTIGATOR: He's got eleven fifty coming in a month.

COMPANY REPRESENTATIVE: Okay. Anything else?

GAO INVESTIGATOR: Well, no, because he's got some — you know, he owns his own house.

COMPANY REPRESENTATIVE: Right. I'm just asking; I don't know your situation.

But eleven fifty a month in Social Security. No other income is coming in.

No savings?

GAO INVESTIGATOR: No, he's got some savings and stuff, but I mean, I'm concerned, again, he's going to lose all that.

COMPANY REPRESENTATIVE: Right.

See, how we work — first of all, I'm accredited by the VA. And what we do is we plug into the software to see what dad qualifies for.

And what we plug into the software is money going in, money going out, money saved, illnesses, what his illness issues are, in other words, what the home health care agency is doing for dad.

All of that plays a major role in crunching the numbers to see what dad qualified for.

And in most cases, [name], it's not a matter of if he qualifies, it's a matter of how much.

Appendix II: Full Transcript of Selected Calls
with Organizations Providing Products and
Services to Help Claimants Qualify for VA
Pension Benefits

GAO INVESTIGATOR: Okay.

COMPANY REPRESENTATIVE: That's going to have to be our next conversation.

I'm just trying to get a little information to see if I can guide you in the right direction.

My question to you regarding the home health care, do you have an idea what they're charging you per month?

GAO INVESTIGATOR: Well, you know, it's probably around a little over two thousand, maybe twenty-five hundred a month.

COMPANY REPRESENTATIVE: Okay. And so here's what you have, [name]. You have more money going out than coming in, as far as income.

GAO INVESTIGATOR: Right.

COMPANY REPRESENTATIVE: So you have a shortfall of about fourteen hundred dollars, thirteen fifty, a month going out for care.

And that's a good thing, when it comes to applying for the VA benefits.

There's other factors, I'm just giving you kind of an overview.

GAO INVESTIGATOR: Okay.

COMPANY REPRESENTATIVE: And it could be, you know, dad may qualify for up to the full nineteen fifty a month.

I don't care if twenty-five hundred is coming in, and twenty-five hundred is going out the door, the software, with all of the bells and whistles of what we have to plug into it, it may kick out that dad needs nineteen fifteen a month.

GAO INVESTIGATOR: Okay, but here's the problem.

COMPANY REPRESENTATIVE: He may have a shortfall of fourteen hundred.

GAO INVESTIGATOR: Yeah, but here's my concern though, is that he's got — he owns his own house, and then he's got like a mutual fund and he's got some savings.

And of course, that's not going to last very long with this negative, you know, income that he's got going on.

COMPANY REPRESENTATIVE: Correct.

GAO INVESTIGATOR: But how is he going to qualify for anything with those assets?

Appendix II: Full Transcript of Selected Calls
with Organizations Providing Products and
Services to Help Claimants Qualify for VA
Pension Benefits

COMPANY REPRESENTATIVE: Well, the VA has different scenarios.

For example, the VA will allow us to do estate planning to reposition the assets so he can qualify.

The VA may be able to allow him to keep a certain amount.

How much money are we talking about in savings or stocks or bonds or mutual funds total?

Just off the top of your head. You don't have to be exact.

GAO INVESTIGATOR: I'm guessing he's got maybe ninety thousand in savings and about two hundred — about a quarter of a million, probably, in mutual funds.

A little over two fifty, two sixty maybe.

COMPANY REPRESENTATIVE: All right. So if he's not opposed, there's like several scenarios.

So let's just talk about money. Those with assets of which we would call your dad.

Is he opposed to repositioning the assets to where — are you the power-of-attorney, [name]?

GAO INVESTIGATOR: Like I say, he's got his mental facilities, so I'm not.

I mean, I could be, but I mean, at this point, he's still able to function for himself.

COMPANY REPRESENTATIVE: Well, your issues here are you have about a quarter of a million dollars plus cash.

The government is going to want him to use his money first, if we don't do estate planning, which we're allowed to do, according to the VA parameters.

GAO INVESTIGATOR: Okay, so what does that mean? Where — what would you do?

COMPANY REPRESENTATIVE: What that means is basically is repositioning the assets to where – it may – and I don't — again, the software tells us what we can and can't do.

But I'm just going to give you a — kind of a hypothetical.

Uh — For example, you may be able to reposition, reallocate those funds into a trust that [name], Jr. — if you're a Jr. – I'll just – [name], you –

GAO INVESTIGATOR: [Inaudible].

**Appendix II: Full Transcript of Selected Calls
with Organizations Providing Products and
Services to Help Claimants Qualify for VA
Pension Benefits**

COMPANY REPRESENTATIVE: — would be the trustee of.

And we're allowed to apply for VA benefits the day after, by reallocating those funds, so that dad can qualify.

And he may get nineteen fifty a month, tax-free, plus retroactive, for the 8 months waiting.

So he may get a full check of about almost twenty something thousand dollars, and the funds thereafter come each month to you tax-free.

Does he want that? I don't know.

Those are some of the scenarios that the software will kick out, and let us know what we can and can't do.

But the bottom line is, if you went to the VA directly and told them — because you would have to be forthright, and tell them that you had this money — they would reject you immediately, until you spend down to your last fifteen hundred dollars.

Or there are options that you could do.

And that's where an accredited VA claims agent comes in, myself, because we work with attorneys that do estate planning that are able to do these type of things.

So those are the questions you want to talk to your dad about, even though he may have his faculties, and he may be able to make decisions.

Is he willing to pull the trigger and let you make the decisions? Because that's what he may have to do.

GAO INVESTIGATOR: Well, I'm just –

COMPANY REPRESENTATIVE: I'm just giving you one of the scenarios.

But our niche is that we deal with people with assets, if they are willing to let the power-of-attorney make those decisions, then we can apply for VA benefits without a hiccup.

GAO INVESTIGATOR: Okay, all right.

COMPANY REPRESENTATIVE: So those are the questions that I probably would talk to my dad about.

GAO INVESTIGATOR: He's pretty reasonable.

COMPANY REPRESENTATIVE: Because quite frankly, there is a gap.

And dad, who knows, can get worse, and then you may have to put him into a nursing — an assisted-living facility, which is twice what you're paying now.

Appendix II: Full Transcript of Selected Calls
with Organizations Providing Products and
Services to Help Claimants Qualify for VA
Pension Benefits

And now it becomes a do or die situation, where do you want to preserve the Estate, or do you want to spend it down?

And those are the questions — those are hard questions to ask.

GAO INVESTIGATOR: Yeah. You know, what I'm seeing now is that those assets are – are dwindling because —

COMPANY REPRESENTATIVE: The economy.

GAO INVESTIGATOR: Yeah, and we're putting out more than, you know, he's only got a little bit coming in with the social security. That's not covering it.

COMPANY REPRESENTATIVE: No, that's right. And what these types of estate planning devices, that's allowed, according to the VA, it's real simple.

I mean, they make it very clear that the — by the way, are you the power-of-attorney?

GAO INVESTIGATOR: I don't have a power-of-attorney, but I can probably get one.

COMPANY REPRESENTATIVE: I would do that yesterday. I would — forget whether we met each other or not. You need to get that done.

What I would suggest — can I make a suggestion?

GAO INVESTIGATOR: Uh-huh.

COMPANY REPRESENTATIVE: Go to Office Depot –

GAO INVESTIGATOR: Yes.

COMPANY REPRESENTATIVE: — get a general power-of-attorney in place. Have a notary notarize it, which will make it legally binding that day of notary.

And now you have a power-of-attorney in place, so that if anything happens to dad, God forbid, he has a stroke and he becomes mentally incapacitated, you've already got something in writing where you can make decisions for him, and you don't have to go through the court system.

GAO INVESTIGATOR: That makes sense.

COMPANY REPRESENTATIVE: So I would do that immediately. And I would tell dad. He wouldn't be opposed to that, would he?

GAO INVESTIGATOR: I don't think so, no. But by the same token, he can still make his own decisions, so I want him to –

Appendix II: Full Transcript of Selected Calls
with Organizations Providing Products and
Services to Help Claimants Qualify for VA
Pension Benefits

COMPANY REPRESENTATIVE: That's doesn't change. I mean, he still makes his own decisions, even with the power-of-attorney in place.

The power-of-attorney is only in case he does become incapacitated.

GAO INVESTIGATOR: Uh-huh.

COMPANY REPRESENTATIVE: Okay. You are basically doing preventive medicine. And that's what we're suggesting here.

If the software kicks out — and I don't know until I get a fact-finder filled out by you in detail, and it's an 8-page fact-finder, it takes me about 7 hours with the attorney to go through all this.

And we don't charge to fill out the VA forms.

We do not charge to represent dad for the VA benefits, but we do charge a flat rate to do the seven hours, eight hours of due diligence to figure out what is going to be the right avenue, because they are only going to have one scenario that's going to fit dad's situation, once we get that fact-finder in.

Because once we get that fact-finder in, the software tells us exactly what we can and can't do.

GAO INVESTIGATOR: All right. And how much is that? What's the cost of that?

COMPANY REPRESENTATIVE: Fifteen hundred dollars.

GAO INVESTIGATOR: Fifteen hundred, okay.

COMPANY REPRESENTATIVE: But it's not a matter of if dad qualifies, it's a matter of how much.

I will tell you, because he's a living vet, our experience from the software, the software will kick back between sixteen to nineteen hundred dollars that he would qualify for, because he's a living vet,. whereas if it was mom, and dad was dead, the surviving spouse always gets less.

GAO INVESTIGATOR: Okay.

COMPANY REPRESENTATIVE: Now if dad qualifies for the nineteen fifty — let's just use that as an example — times, ah, he'll get a check on the ninth month, if we apply for it yesterday, and got everything in place, he would get a check from the government for seventeen thousand five hundred fifty dollars, tax-free.

And then, each month thereafter, he would get nineteen fifty coming in, each month, tax-free.

GAO INVESTIGATOR: Whoa.

Appendix II: Full Transcript of Selected Calls
with Organizations Providing Products and
Services to Help Claimants Qualify for VA
Pension Benefits

COMPANY REPRESENTATIVE: That's how that works. I'm here to tell you, that for fifteen hundred dollars, you'll get your money back on the first month that you apply, basically.

GAO INVESTIGATOR: Yeah, yeah.

COMPANY REPRESENTATIVE: But once we do what we need to do, and if he's not objected — objecting to the reallocating and repositioning of those funds, because quite frankly, at 86, I know he has two hundred and fifty thousand in mutual funds, but you know, that's a concern to me right there, because of the loss and what's going on in the economy.

GAO INVESTIGATOR: Uh-huh.

COMPANY REPRESENTATIVE: So is he willing to pull the trigger and get it out of harm's way, so that he would get between 4 to 6 percent, and not — and not at any risk?

Because if we do reposition the funds, it's very likely that it has to be an account that cannot go backwards.

GAO INVESTIGATOR: All right. So what type of thing are you talking about?

COMPANY REPRESENTATIVE: It could be CDs, it could be annuities, but the point is, it has to be an account that's protected, that can't go backwards.

There's not an attorney, that I know that's accredited, that would will take any case that's going to be tied into stocks, bonds, or mutual funds, because they can lose their base, they can lose their principal, they can lose their gains.

And the attorney signs off on that stuff, when he represents the VA.

GAO INVESTIGATOR: Okay. And if he's putting it into something, and he's getting 4 to 6 percent, does that money go to him or where does that go?

COMPANY REPRESENTATIVE: If it stays into the account, it goes to him.

How it works, basically, [name], it's that the power-of-attorney is the decision maker with dad.

You become the trustee.

GAO INVESTIGATOR: Okay.

COMPANY REPRESENTATIVE: You are the pivot, you are the person we go to.

Because everything has to be reallocated out of dad's name, titled to the trust, so that [name] controls it, [name] cuts the checks.

**Appendix II: Full Transcript of Selected Calls
with Organizations Providing Products and
Services to Help Claimants Qualify for VA
Pension Benefits**

Dad's allowed to keep money in his account, that's not a question. It's a question of how much is he allowed to keep in his account.

That depends on the software coming back and telling us what he's allowed to keep, what he's not allowed to keep.

GAO INVESTIGATOR: Uh-huh, uh-huh.

COMPANY REPRESENTATIVE: Do you follow?

GAO INVESTIGATOR: If I use any of that money for him or for me, I have to count that as income?

COMPANY REPRESENTATIVE: Great question. Let's talk about for him first.

If you use the money for him — first of all, the Trust will Dad has what? — am I correct by saying he has over two fifty, combined, like three forty?

GAO INVESTIGATOR: Yeah. Well, like I say, he's got about ninety in savings and another two — maybe about two sixty in a mutual fund.

COMPANY REPRESENTATIVE: So three fifty he has total.

GAO INVESTIGATOR: Okay, yeah.

COMPANY REPRESENTATIVE: So what would happen, in this Trust account, visualize it as there's a checkbook access.

In the checkbook access, you're able — you're going to have up to three fifty, what's going to be liquid is going to be roughly about close to a hundred and fifty thousand dollars, or a hundred thousand minimum.

GAO INVESTIGATOR: Okay.

COMPANY REPRESENTATIVE: So that's for incidentals, for dad's needs, for whatever. It doesn't make a difference.

I don't have to know what it's for.

GAO INVESTIGATOR: Okay. But if I use that, does somebody, either I or him, have to count that as income?

COMPANY REPRESENTATIVE: Well, if he cashes in his – are these IRAs? Do you know?

GAO INVESTIGATOR: Well, no. I mean –

COMPANY REPRESENTATIVE: Okay. If they're not IRAs, and they're just non-IRAs, non-401(k)s, non-retirement plans –

Appendix II: Full Transcript of Selected Calls
with Organizations Providing Products and
Services to Help Claimants Qualify for VA
Pension Benefits

GAO INVESTIGATOR: Right.

COMPANY REPRESENTATIVE: — then, no, you could use them into the account —, and they could be taxable— for whatever, it's not countable as income.

But if they are IRAs, then you would have to cash in the IRAs and then it would become income.

GAO INVESTIGATOR: Okay.

COMPANY REPRESENTATIVE: But the other account, when it's put into the put and keep account — let's say you have three hundred and fifty thousand.

A hundred to a hundred fifty goes into the checkbook access.

The other two hundred or whatever goes into a put and keep account earning four to six percent.

GAO INVESTIGATOR: Is that like an annuity or something?

COMPANY REPRESENTATIVE: That doesn't earn any interest. That's accessible dollars, liquid dollars, when you need it for emergency.

The other account will earn 4 to 6 percent.

So it depends on what you want to put into that other account, and how much you want to keep liquid.

GAO INVESTIGATOR: Okay. Well, the account that's earning 4 to 6 percent, what is that in? Is that an annuity or what is that?

COMPANY REPRESENTATIVE: It would be an annuity that has accessibility to it, but it's tax-free, it's not being — it's not being taxed.

GAO INVESTIGATOR: Okay. All right. But I wouldn't have access to that money?

COMPANY REPRESENTATIVE: You will have access to that money. Each year you have access to it, up to 10 percent free withdrawal, with no penalty.

GAO INVESTIGATOR: Okay.

COMPANY REPRESENTATIVE: And if — but that's why we want to keep some of that money out in the Trust account checkbook, that is basically accessible, totally liquid.

So the software will kick out what we can and can't do.

I'm projecting that probably a hundred and fifty of it, up to a hundred and fifty, could be liquid.

Appendix II: Full Transcript of Selected Calls
with Organizations Providing Products and
Services to Help Claimants Qualify for VA
Pension Benefits

Now you may not need a hundred and fifty liquid. So the more you put into the annuity, the more interest you're going to earn on those funds.

GAO INVESTIGATOR: Uh-huh.

COMPANY REPRESENTATIVE: That's a decision you have to make with dad.

GAO INVESTIGATOR: Okay.

COMPANY REPRESENTATIVE: But from my experience on the software, I've seen between, - a hundred and fifty or a hundred thousand go into the annuity — checking account, and the rest goes into the annuity.

GAO INVESTIGATOR: Uh-huh.

Well, hopefully, you're talking this VA thing.

Is that really — the nineteen or whatever that he would qualify for, is that a pension or what is that?

COMPANY REPRESENTATIVE: It's — it's — I'm sorry. It's going to be considered what is called Aid and Attendance.

GAO INVESTIGATOR: Okay.

COMPANY REPRESENTATIVE: It's aiding him with him attendance for his care, and that is the home health care.

Remember, I mentioned that there's three things that have to be in place in order for us even to apply for the VA benefits called Aid and Attendance.

And that he is already getting aid, you know, from a home health care, or assisted-living or in a nursing home.

GAO INVESTIGATOR: Uh-huh. All right.

COMPANY REPRESENTATIVE: And so we're applying for specifically that. That's all I deal with.

I don't deal with any of the other benefits that the VA has.

GAO INVESTIGATOR: Okay. All right, all right.

COMPANY REPRESENTATIVE: But you do have some obstacles. You have some issues that you need to discuss with dad.

If you're interested, I believe that it's a fit.

It's not a matter of if he qualifies, it's a matter of how much. But the computer will tell us what we can and can't do.

And then, if you like, I can e-mail you the fact-finder and the information. There's two forms I would send to you that you would send back to me, signed, with a check, and the address is on the fact-finder.

If you like, I can e-mail it to you, if you have an e-mail address.

GAO INVESTIGATOR: I'll tell you what, I want to talk to him about it first.

COMPANY REPRESENTATIVE: Okay, great. Just keep us in mind. You have our number; give us a call.

GAO INVESTIGATOR: Okay. I'm trying to think if I have any other questions for you. I was just trying to write down a couple things here.

All right, I mean, I guess that's it.

COMPANY REPRESENTATIVE: The problem that you have right now is that you have assets.

We have to definitely — I know, from experience, that if you have assets, there may be a strong possibility of repositioning some of those assets.

And there's a way to reposition some to the trust and there's a way to reposition some to dad, and there's a way to reposition to [name].

GAO INVESTIGATOR: Right, right.

COMPANY REPRESENTATIVE: That all comes from the software, once it kicks it out.

GAO INVESTIGATOR: All right. And you said that the cost is fifteen hundred bucks for the —

COMPANY REPRESENTATIVE: Flat rate, yeah, no extra costs.

GAO INVESTIGATOR: All right. Well, let me talk to him and I'll get back to you.

COMPANY REPRESENTATIVE: All right. Nice meeting you, [name].

GAO INVESTIGATOR: Thank you for your time.

COMPANY REPRESENTATIVE: Bye bye.

Appendix III: Comments from the Department of Veterans Affairs

DEPARTMENT OF VETERANS AFFAIRS
Washington DC 20420

May 8, 2012

Daniel Bertoni
Director, Education, Workforce
  and Income Security Issues
U.S. Government Accountability Office
441 G Street, NW
Washington, DC 20548

Dear Mr. Bertoni:

The Department of Veterans Affairs (VA) has reviewed the Government Accountability Office's (GAO) draft report, *"VETERANS' PENSION BENEFITS: Improvements Needed to Ensure Only Qualified Veterans and Survivors Receive Benefits"* (GAO-12-540). VA generally agrees with GAO's conclusions and concurs with three recommendations and concurs in principle with one recommendation to the Department.

The enclosure specifically addresses GAO's recommendations and provides general and technical comments to the draft report. VA appreciates the opportunity to comment on your draft report.

Sincerely,

John R. Gingrich
Chief of Staff

Enclosure

Enclosure

Department of Veterans Affairs (VA) Comments to
Government Accountability Office (GAO) Draft Report:
*"VETERANS' PENSION BENEFITS: Improvements Needed to Ensure
Only Qualified Veterans and Survivors Receive Benefits"*
(GAO-12-540)

VA's General Comments: Before addressing GAO's specific recommendations, VA
offers comments regarding GAO's conclusion that the design and management of the
pension program fails to ensure that this needs-based benefit is being provided to only
those Veterans and survivors with a demonstrated need. VA's improved pension
program was designed by Congress to provide economic security to financially
disadvantaged wartime Veterans and their survivors without undue delay. Accordingly,
from the program's inception in 1979, VA's implementation has focused on paying
pension benefits quickly and without the extensive development of evidence often
required in VA's disability compensation program. Operating under this framework, VA
paid in fiscal year 2011 over $4.2 billion in pension benefits to over 313,000 Veterans
and 203,000 survivors. During that year alone, VA completed nearly 50,000 original
claims for Veterans' pension and over 60,000 claims for survivors' pension, while
maintaining an accuracy rate of nearly 98%.

Because of their financial need and often advanced age, pension recipients are among
the Department's most vulnerable beneficiaries. These beneficiaries comprise more
than 50% of the individuals in VA's fiduciary program for beneficiaries who cannot
manage their VA benefits as a result of injury, disease, or the infirmities of age.
Recognizing this, last year the Secretary of Veterans Affairs authorized a reorganization
within the Veterans Benefits Administration (VBA) to establish a new office to more
directly control and administer the Department's pension program. In April 2011, VBA
established the Pension and Fiduciary (P&F) Service, led by a VA Senior Executive, to
focus, in part, on the unique needs of the pension program and pension beneficiaries.
This reorganization has allowed VBA to increase the staff responsible for pension policy
and procedures, and to establish a separate staff responsible for all aspects of pension
quality, training, and program oversight.

One of the first tasks undertaken by the new P&F Service in January 2012, was to
identify gaps in VA's pension regulations, particularly with respect to program integrity
measures. P&F Service identified gaps in VA's regulations, including a lack of a
prescribed look-back period for asset transfers, and a lack of specific regulations
addressing the use of trusts and annuities for purposes of reducing net worth and
creating pension eligibility. The Service noted that the forward-looking nature of the
pension application process, combined with the lack of specific rules governing asset
transfers, produced circumstances in which one claimant could transfer substantial
assets to another person before applying for pension and still receive the benefit, while
a similarly-situated pension beneficiary in possession of the same assets would not be
eligible for pension due to excessive net worth. Accordingly, P&F Service began
drafting regulations to address these and other issues related to the integrity of the
pension program.

1

Department of Veterans Affairs (VA) Comments to
Government Accountability Office (GAO) Draft Report:
*"VETERANS' PENSION BENEFITS: Improvements Needed to Ensure
Only Qualified Veterans and Survivors Receive Benefits"*
(GAO-12-540)

Despite the need to impose additional program integrity measures, which may add
complexity to the pension adjudication process, VBA remains committed to delivering
this needs-based benefit as quickly as possible to wartime Veterans and their survivors.
To offset the potential for added complexity, VBA has also been working on ways to
expedite the adjudication of pension claims, to include permitting a family member to
submit verification of income and eligibility information to VA on behalf of an elderly
claimant and developing an automated rules-based processing system for pension
claims.

Throughout the report, GAO compares VA's pension program to other Federal needs-
based programs, specifically the Department of Health and Human Services' Medicaid
program and the Social Security Administration's Supplemental Security Income (SSI)
program. However, as GAO's report correctly notes, unlike Medicaid and SSI, the
statutes governing VA's pension program lack provisions addressing the effects of
transfers of assets on eligibility for program benefits, e.g., a look-back and penalty
period. Although VBA is working to prescribe such provisions in regulations, it will have
to follow the rulemaking procedures required by Congress in the Administrative
Procedure Act and the resulting regulations will be subject to challenge in the U.S.
Court of Appeals for the Federal Circuit. VA notes that the GAO report also
recommends that Congress enact legislation to establish a look-back and penalty period
for pension claimants who transfer assets in an attempt to create eligibility.

**GAO Recommendation: To improve VA's ability to ensure that only veterans and
surviving spouses with financial need receive VA pension benefits, the Secretary
of Veterans Affairs should direct the Undersecretary for Benefits to take the
following actions:**

Recommendation 1: Modify pension application forms, as well as eligibility verification
report forms, to include space for claimants or recipients to report asset transfers, and
to specify annuities, trusts, or private retirement income. For assets, such as annuities
and trusts that are reported, forms should also request related documentation to enable
claims processors to determine if claimants or recipients retain ownership and control of
these assets.

VA Response: Concur. As part of the ongoing pension improvement initiatives
described above, VBA is revising pension forms to ensure they provide the necessary
space for pension applicants and beneficiaries to report assets, asset transfers, and
retirement income. While VBA agrees that the forms need additional space and
instructions, VBA also recognizes that lengthy and complex benefit application forms
may have the unintended effect of deterring Veterans and survivors from applying for

2

Enclosure

Department of Veterans Affairs (VA) Comments to
Government Accountability Office (GAO) Draft Report:
*"VETERANS' PENSION BENEFITS: Improvements Needed to Ensure
Only Qualified Veterans and Survivors Receive Benefits"*
(GAO-12-540)

pension. Accordingly, in revising the current forms, VBA will balance the need for
program integrity with the need for forms that do not impose an undue burden on these
often-elderly claimants. In addition, VBA will revise the instructions for pension-related
forms to direct claimants and beneficiaries to provide additional evidence for purposes
of enabling VA to determine ownership and control of assets transferred using annuities
and trusts.

Recommendation 2: For all claimants, verify financial information during the initial
claims assessment process. This may include requesting supporting documentation
such as bank statements and tax returns, or using automated databases that can verify
financial information.

VA Response: Concur in principle. VBA notes that GAO did not provide any data
regarding the costs or benefits associated with additional up-front verification of a
claimant's financial information. Because VA's goal is to decide claims within 125 days,
while maintaining a high-level of accuracy, and because verification of financial
information during the initial adjudication process will add to the time required to decide
pension claims, VBA will analyze the issue and determine how best to conduct an up-
front verification of financial information. This analysis will consider whether VA can
exclude applicants who do not have the need prescribed by Congress without adding
undue burden to genuine pension claimants and beneficiaries, many of whom are
advanced in age. Anticipated completion date is November 1, 2012.

Recommendation 3: Strengthen coordination between pension and fiduciary programs
to identify pension claimants or recipients who have transferred or unreported assets,
such as allowing claims processors access to fiduciary field exam reports for these
cases.

VA Response: Concur. VBA currently conducts more than 70,000 fiduciary field
examinations annually. According to VBA's Adjudication Procedures Manual, M21-
1MR, Part XI.4.C.11.a, fiduciary program personnel must immediately provide Pension
Management Center (PMC) personnel with information that may establish a basis for
adjusting a beneficiary's pension benefit. This process ensures program integrity
without requiring PMC personnel to review every field examination report generated by
VBA's fiduciary activities. It also allows VBA's fiduciary field examiners to assess the
credibility of information they obtain from multiple sources, to include incompetent
beneficiaries and their family members and other acquaintances, and determine
whether it could affect pension eligibility. VBA has effective procedures in place for
coordination between the pension and fiduciary programs regarding benefit adjustments
and other benefit matters. In addition, VBA has established a pension-fiduciary

3

Enclosure

Department of Veterans Affairs (VA) Comments to
Government Accountability Office (GAO) Draft Report:
*"VETERANS' PENSION BENEFITS: Improvements Needed to Ensure
Only Qualified Veterans and Survivors Receive Benefits"*
(GAO-12-540)

workgroup, which meets monthly to discuss methods for improving program
coordination. This group is establishing procedures to further facilitate the receipt of
income information from fiduciary to pension personnel to strengthen coordination.
Based on all of our current efforts and the refinement of income information transfer, we
recommend that GAO close this recommendation.

Recommendation 4: Revise the VA procedures manual to better define the concept of
ownership and control to help claims processors determine when specific types of
assets such as annuities and trusts should be counted as part of net worth, and
establish a more specific criteria for what is considered a reasonable period of time for
pension claimants to use up their financial resources before becoming eligible for
pension benefits.

VA Response: Concur. However, rather than initially revising its Adjudication
Procedures Manual, which is not binding on claimants, VBA is drafting proposed
regulations that would address the effect of pre-filing asset transfers on pension
eligibility. These regulations would also address and clarify the various factors VA uses
to determine whether excessive net worth precludes eligibility for pension, e.g., life
expectancy, income, expenses, and liquidity of assets, and generally provide a more
consistent set of rules for adjudicating pension claims. Upon completion of the
rulemaking proceeding, VBA will amend its manual provisions consistent with the new
regulations. The amended manual will interpret the regulations and provide the
procedures required to properly implement them. Anticipated completion date is
December 1, 2013.

4

Appendix IV: GAO Contact and Staff Acknowledgments

GAO Contact	Daniel Bertoni, (202) 512-7215 or bertonid@gao.gov.
Staff Acknowledgments	In addition to the contact named above, individuals making key contributions to this report were Jeremy Cox, Assistant Director; James Bennett; Susannah Compton; Paul Desaulniers; Shelia Drake; Alex Galuten; Douglas Manor; Nelson Olhero; Martin Scire; Wayne Turowski; Walter Vance, and Gregory Whitney

Related GAO Products

VA Enhanced Monthly Benefits: Recipient Population Is Changing and Awareness Could be Improved. GAO-12-153. Washington D.C.: December 14, 2011.

VA's Fiduciary Program: VA Plans to Improve Program Compliance and Policies, but Sustained Management Attention is Needed. GAO-10-635T. Washington, D.C.: April 22, 2010.

VA's Fiduciary Program: Improved Compliance and Policies Could Better Safeguard Veterans' Benefits. GAO-10-241. Washington, D.C.: February 26, 2010.

Veterans' Benefits: Improved Management Would Enhance VA's Pension Program. GAO-08-112. Washington, D.C.: February 14, 2008.

Medicaid Long Term Care: Few Transferred Assets before Applying for Nursing Home Coverage; Impact of Deficit Reduction Act on Eligibility Is Uncertain. GAO-07-280. Washington D.C.: March 26, 2007.

Medicaid: Transfer of Assets by Elderly Individuals to Obtain Long-Term Care Coverage. GAO-05-968. Washington D.C.: September 2, 2005.